Learn Python From an Expert V2

© 2023 by Edson L P Camacho

Dedication

It was a battle to write a book of this size and with this expert content, to deliver the best there is for Python language users.

My family was my support, I want to thank my wife Vanessa, my son Giovanni and my God for giving me strength to complete this project.

I offer it to all my readers, and I thank everyone for trusting the information contained in this book, as support for the solutions they may eventually have.

This is a great journey, only the strong and those who don't give up make it to the end, I wish you all success!

One day the prophet Isaiah said...

"All men are like grass and all their glory is like the flowers of the field... The grass withers and the flowers fall, but the Word of our God stands forever."

Isaiah 40: 7-8

Edson L P Camacho

Table of Contents

○ Important introduction to Python

Why use the Python language

There are many reasons why Python is a popular and widely used language for various applications, such as:

Easy to learn: Python has a simple and intuitive syntax that makes it easy to learn for beginners. The language emphasizes readability and clarity, which makes it easier to understand and maintain code.

Versatility: Python can be used for a wide range of applications, including web development, scientific computing, artificial intelligence, machine learning, data analysis, and more.

Large community and extensive libraries: Python has a large and active community of developers, which means there is a wealth of resources and support available online. There are also many libraries and frameworks available that make it easier to develop applications in Python.

Cross-platform compatibility: Python can be run on various operating systems, including Windows, macOS, and Linux, making it a versatile language for development.

Rapid prototyping: Python's simplicity and ease of use make it a popular choice for rapid prototyping and development of minimum viable products (MVPs).

High demand and career opportunities: Python is one of the most in-demand programming languages in the job market, and it offers various career opportunities for developers, data scientists, and AI/ML professionals.

Overall, Python is a powerful and flexible language that is well-suited for a wide range of applications and industries. Its simplicity, versatility, and large community make it an excellent choice for both beginners and experienced developers.

Python is considered easy to learn for several reasons:

1. Simple and readable syntax: Python has a simple and intuitive syntax that emphasizes readability and reduces the complexity of the code. The language uses plain English words and a minimalist design that makes it easy to understand and write code.

2. Fewer lines of code: Python requires fewer lines of code to accomplish the same task as other programming languages, which reduces the time and effort required to write, test, and maintain code.

3. Extensive documentation and community support: Python has a large and active community of developers who contribute to its development and maintenance. This community provides extensive documentation, tutorials, and resources that make it easier for beginners to learn and use Python.

4. Interactive mode: Python allows developers to enter code interactively and see the results immediately, which provides instant feedback and makes it easier to experiment and learn.

5. Versatility: Python can be used for a wide range of applications, from web development and data analysis to machine learning and scientific computing. Its versatility makes it easier for developers to find applications and projects that interest them.

Overall, Python's simplicity, readability, and versatility make it a popular choice for beginners and experienced developers alike. The language's ease of use and extensive community support make it easier for developers to learn, use, and master Python.

Is Python versatility?

Yes, Python is a versatile programming language that can be used for a wide range of applications. Python's versatility comes from the fact that it is a general-purpose language that can be used for many different purposes, including:

Web development: Python is commonly used for web development, with popular frameworks such as Django and Flask.

Data analysis and visualization: Python has a wide range of libraries and tools for data analysis and visualization, such as NumPy, Pandas, and Matplotlib.

Scientific computing: Python is widely used in scientific computing, with libraries such as SciPy, SymPy, and Biopython.

Artificial intelligence and machine learning: Python is one of the most popular languages for machine learning and AI, with libraries such as TensorFlow, Keras, and PyTorch.

Desktop applications: Python can be used to develop desktop applications using frameworks such as PyQt and PyGTK.

Game development: Python can be used for game development, with libraries such as Pygame.

Automation and scripting: Python is commonly used for automation and scripting tasks, such as system administration, network programming, and web scraping.

Overall, Python's versatility makes it a popular choice for a wide range of applications and industries, from startups and small businesses to large enterprises and scientific research institutions.

Python with large community and extensive libraries

Python has a large and active community of developers and users, which is one of its biggest strengths. The community is constantly contributing to the development and improvement of Python, and there is a wealth of resources and support available online.

In addition to its community, Python also has an extensive library of modules and packages that can be used for various purposes. These libraries include:

1. NumPy: a library for numerical computing and scientific computing.
2. Pandas: a library for data manipulation and analysis.
3. Matplotlib: a library for creating visualizations and plots.
4. Scikit-learn: a library for machine learning and data mining.
5. TensorFlow: a library for deep learning and neural networks.
6. Flask and Django: web development frameworks that are widely used for building web applications.
7. Pygame: a library for game development.
8. BeautifulSoup: a library for web scraping.
9. Requests: a library for making HTTP requests.
10. Pytest: a testing framework for Python.

These libraries and packages make it easier for developers to build complex applications and solve challenging problems. They also help to reduce the amount of time and effort required to develop and maintain code.

Overall, Python's large community and extensive library of modules and packages make it a powerful and versatile language that is well-suited for a wide range of applications and industries.

Where is python used nowadays?

Python is used in a wide range of industries and applications. Some of the most common uses of Python include:

1. Web development: Python is widely used for web development, with popular frameworks such as Django, Flask, and Pyramid.
2. Data analysis and visualization: Python has a variety of libraries and tools for data analysis and visualization, including Pandas, NumPy, Matplotlib, and Seaborn.
3. Machine learning and artificial intelligence: Python is one of the most popular languages for machine learning and AI, with popular libraries such as TensorFlow, Keras, and Scikit-learn.
4. Scientific computing: Python is widely used in scientific computing, with libraries such as SciPy, SymPy, and Biopython.
5. Desktop applications: Python can be used to develop desktop applications using frameworks such as PyQt and wxPython.
6. Game development: Python can be used for game development, with libraries such as Pygame.
7. Automation and scripting: Python is commonly used for automation and scripting tasks, such as system administration, network programming, and web scraping.
8. Education: Python is often used as an introductory programming language in education, as its simplicity and readability make it easy for beginners to learn.
9. Finance: Python is widely used in finance for data analysis, algorithmic trading, and risk management.
10. DevOps: Python is used for automation and orchestration in DevOps, with popular tools such as Ansible, Salt, and Fabric.

Overall, Python's versatility and ease of use make it a popular choice for developers in many different industries and applications. Its large community and extensive library of modules and packages also make it a powerful language for solving complex problems and building robust applications.

What can we do with the Python language?

Python is a versatile programming language that can be used for a wide variety of tasks and applications. Here are some examples of what you can do with Python:

1. Web development: Python can be used to create web applications using popular frameworks such as Django, Flask, and Pyramid.
2. Data analysis and visualization: Python has a range of libraries and tools for data analysis and visualization, such as Pandas, NumPy, Matplotlib, and Seaborn.

3. Machine learning and artificial intelligence: Python is one of the most popular languages for machine learning and AI, with libraries such as TensorFlow, Keras, Scikit-learn, and PyTorch.Scientific computing: Python is widely used in scientific computing, with libraries such as SciPy, SymPy, and Biopython.
4. Desktop applications: Python can be used to develop desktop applications using frameworks such as PyQt and wxPython.
5. Game development: Python can be used for game development, with libraries such as Pygame.
6. Automation and scripting: Python is commonly used for automation and scripting tasks, such as system administration, network programming, and web scraping.
7. Education: Python is often used as an introductory programming language in education, as its simplicity and readability make it easy for beginners to learn.
8. Finance: Python is widely used in finance for data analysis, algorithmic trading, and risk management.
9. DevOps: Python is used for automation and orchestration in DevOps, with popular tools such as Ansible, Salt, and Fabric.

Overall, Python is a powerful language that can be used for a wide range of tasks and applications. Its versatility and ease of use make it a popular choice for developers in many different industries and domains.

What is the downside of using Python?

While Python is a powerful and versatile language, it does have some limitations and drawbacks. Here are some potential downsides to using Python:

Performance: Python is an interpreted language, which means it can be slower than compiled languages like C or Java. This can make it less suitable for certain types of high-performance applications, such as real-time systems or resource-intensive tasks.

GIL: Python has a Global Interpreter Lock (GIL), which can limit its ability to take full advantage of multi-core processors. This can make it less suitable for certain types of CPU-bound tasks.

Memory management: Python uses automatic memory management, which can lead to performance issues if memory usage is not carefully managed. This can be a problem for applications that need to process large amounts of data.

Version compatibility: Python has multiple versions, and not all libraries or frameworks are compatible with every version. This can create compatibility issues and make it difficult to maintain code over time.

Packaging: Python's packaging system can be complex and difficult to manage, especially for large projects with many dependencies.

Security: Python is a popular language, which can make it a target for security vulnerabilities and attacks.

Overall, while Python has many advantages, it may not be the best choice for every application or use case. Developers should carefully consider their requirements and constraints before deciding to use Python.

What does Python do?

Python in System Programming

Python is a versatile programming language used for various tasks, including system programming. Python's popularity stems from its flexibility and readability, making it an ideal language for system programming. In this article, we'll explore what Python does in system programming and its benefits.

Overview of System Programming

System programming involves creating software that interacts with the hardware and operating system of a computer. It's a low-level task that requires developers to have a good understanding of the computer's architecture and how it interacts with the operating system. System programming is often used to create system utilities, device drivers, and operating systems.

Python in System Programming

Python is a high-level language that has been gaining popularity in system programming. Despite being a high-level language, it still offers low-level programming capabilities that make it an ideal language for system programming. Python's extensive standard library provides developers with access to a wide range of system functionalities, making it easier to write system programs.

Python's Benefits in System Programming

Python has several benefits in system programming, including:

Easy to Learn: Python is an easy-to-learn language that can be used by both novice and experienced developers. It's a high-level language with simple syntax and semantics that make it easy to read and write code.

Cross-Platform Compatibility: Python is a cross-platform language that can run on different operating systems, including Windows, Linux, and macOS. This makes it easier to develop system programs that can run on different platforms without the need for additional software.

Large Community: Python has a large community of developers who contribute to its development and share their knowledge and expertise. This community provides support and resources to developers, making it easier to find help and solutions to problems.

Extensive Libraries: Python has an extensive standard library that provides developers with access to various functionalities for system programming. These libraries make it easier to write system programs without the need for additional code.

Conclusion

Python has become a popular language in system programming due to its flexibility, ease of use, and extensive libraries. Python's ability to run on different operating systems and its large community of developers make it an ideal language for system programming. Its simplicity and low-level capabilities make it an easy language to learn for both novice and experienced developers. As the demand for system programming continues to grow, Python's role in this field is expected to increase.

Python in Digital Games

Python is a popular programming language used for a wide range of applications. One of the areas where Python has made a significant impact is in digital games development. Python is used to create games of all types, from simple 2D platformers to complex 3D simulations.

The popularity of Python in the digital games industry can be attributed to its simplicity, versatility, and flexibility. Python's syntax is easy to read and understand, making it accessible to both new and experienced developers. Python's ability to integrate with other programming languages and software tools also makes it a popular choice for game development.

Python in Data Mining

Data mining is the process of analyzing and extracting meaningful patterns and insights from large datasets. Python is a powerful tool for data mining and has become a go-to language for many data scientists and analysts.

Python's simplicity, ease of use, and powerful libraries such as NumPy, Pandas, and Scikit-learn, make it ideal for data mining tasks. These libraries provide a range of data analysis and visualization tools that allow developers to process and analyze data quickly and efficiently.

Python in Robotics

Python is also widely used in robotics programming. Robotics is the branch of technology that deals with the design, construction, operation, and application of robots. Python's simplicity and versatility make it an ideal language for robotics programming.

Python's ease of use and readability make it a popular choice for beginners looking to learn robotics programming. Python's extensive library ecosystem also provides developers with a range of tools and frameworks for robotics programming, such as PyRobot, ROS, and TensorFlow.

Python in Image Processing

Image processing is the process of manipulating and analyzing digital images using algorithms. Python is a popular language for image processing due to its simplicity, powerful libraries, and versatility.

Python's libraries such as OpenCV, Pillow, and Scikit-image provide developers with a range of tools for image processing, such as image filtering, edge detection, and object recognition. These tools can be used in a variety of applications, from medical imaging to facial recognition.

Conclusion

Python is a versatile and powerful programming language that has made significant contributions to many areas of technology, including digital games, data mining, robotics, and image processing. Python's simplicity, ease of use, and powerful libraries have made it a popular choice for developers looking to create powerful and efficient applications in these areas. Whether you're a beginner or an experienced developer, Python has something to offer for everyone.

• Python and Database Programming

Python is a popular programming language that has gained a lot of popularity in recent years due to its simplicity, flexibility, and ease of use. One of the areas in which Python has made significant inroads is database programming. In this article, we will discuss what Python does with database programming and how it is used to develop robust, scalable, and efficient database applications.

Python and Database Connectivity

Python provides an extensive library of modules for database connectivity. These modules allow programmers to connect to a wide range of databases, such as MySQL, PostgreSQL, Oracle, and Microsoft SQL Server, among others. The modules provide an API for performing common database operations such as querying, updating, and inserting data. These modules provide a convenient way of interacting with databases from within Python programs, without the need for writing complex SQL statements.

Python and Data Modeling

Python is also widely used for data modeling in database programming. Python provides an object-relational mapping (ORM) framework that allows developers to map object-oriented data models to relational databases. This framework simplifies the development of database applications by eliminating the need for writing complex SQL statements. The ORM framework also provides features such as lazy loading, caching, and optimistic locking, which can help improve the performance of database applications.

Python and Database Administration

Python is also used for database administration tasks. Python provides modules for managing databases, such as creating and deleting tables, backing up and restoring databases, and managing user accounts. These modules provide a convenient way of automating database administration tasks, which can help reduce errors and increase productivity.

Python and Data Analysis

Python is widely used for data analysis in database programming. Python provides powerful libraries for data analysis, such as NumPy, Pandas, and Matplotlib, among others. These libraries provide a convenient way of analyzing large amounts of data and generating meaningful insights. Python can also be used for data mining and machine learning tasks, which can help organizations gain a competitive advantage by predicting trends and making informed decisions.

Python and Big Data

Python is also used for big data applications in database programming. Python provides libraries such as PySpark and Dask, which allow developers to work with big data technologies

such as Hadoop, Spark, and NoSQL databases. These libraries provide a convenient way of processing large amounts of data in parallel, which can help improve the performance of big data applications.

Conclusion

Python is a versatile programming language that is widely used in database programming. Python provides extensive libraries for database connectivity, data modeling, database administration, data analysis, and big data applications. Python's simplicity, flexibility, and ease of use make it an ideal choice for developing robust, scalable, and efficient database applications.

Python and GUIs

Python is a general-purpose programming language that is widely used for web development, data analysis, and scientific computing. It has also proven to be a popular choice for building graphical user interfaces (GUIs) due to its simplicity and ease of use. Python has several GUI toolkits available that make it easy to create GUI applications for various platforms and operating systems. In this article, we will explore how Python is used in GUI programming and some of the popular Python GUI toolkits.

GUI Toolkits in Python

There are several GUI toolkits available in Python, each with its own strengths and weaknesses. Here are some of the most popular ones:

1. Tkinter: Tkinter is the standard GUI toolkit that comes bundled with Python. It is a lightweight toolkit and is very easy to use. Tkinter provides a wide range of widgets, such as buttons, labels, and text boxes, which can be used to create simple to moderately complex GUI applications.
2. PyQt: PyQt is a set of Python bindings for the popular C++ Qt toolkit. It is a powerful and feature-rich toolkit that provides a wide range of widgets, such as buttons, menus, and text boxes, as well as support for advanced features like drag and drop, database integration, and multimedia.
3. wxPython: wxPython is a Python wrapper for the C++ wxWidgets toolkit. It is a cross-platform toolkit that provides native look and feel for each platform. wxPython provides a wide range of widgets and advanced features like database integration, drag and drop, and multimedia.
4. Kivy: Kivy is an open-source Python library for developing mobile and desktop applications. It provides a comprehensive set of widgets, such as buttons, text boxes, and sliders, as well as support for advanced features like multitouch, graphics, and animations.

GUI Programming with Tkinter

As mentioned earlier, Tkinter is the standard GUI toolkit that comes bundled with Python. It is a lightweight toolkit and is very easy to use. Here is a simple example of how to create a GUI application using Tkinter:

```python
import tkinter as tk

def say_hello():
    print("Hello, World!")

root = tk.Tk()
root.geometry("200x200")

btn = tk.Button(root, text="Click Me", command=say_hello)
btn.pack()
root.mainloop()
```

In the above example, we import the tkinter module and define a function that prints "Hello, World!" when called. We then create a Tk object, set its geometry, and create a button widget that calls the say_hello function when clicked. Finally, we pack the button widget and start the main event loop.

GUI Programming with PyQt

PyQt provides a more powerful and feature-rich toolkit compared to Tkinter. Here is a simple example of how to create a GUI application using PyQt:

```python
import sys
```

```python
from PyQt5.QtWidgets import QApplication, QMainWindow, QPushButton

class MyWindow(QMainWindow):
    def __init__(self):
        super().__init__()

        self.setGeometry(100, 100, 300, 300)
        self.setWindowTitle("My Window")

        btn = QPushButton("Click Me", self)
        btn.setGeometry(100, 100, 100, 30)
        btn.clicked.connect(self.say_hello)

    def say_hello(self):
        print("Hello, World!")

app = QApplication(sys.argv)
window = MyWindow()
window.show()
sys.exit(app.exec_())
```

In the above example, we import the necessary modules from PyQt5 and define a custom QMainWindow class. We set its geometry and title, create a button widget that calls the say_hello function when clicked, and show the main window.

Python was created in 1989 by Guido van Rossum, and first released on February 20, 1991. Its design philosophy emphasizes code readability and simplicity. It is a high-level, interpreted language and is widely used in web development, data analysis, artificial intelligence, and more. Its popularity is due to its easy-to-learn syntax and vast collection of libraries and frameworks.

• Running programs with Python

Introduction to Python Interpreter: Understanding the Core of Python

Python is a popular, high-level programming language that is widely used in software development, data analysis, and scientific computing. Python's design philosophy emphasizes code readability, and its syntax allows programmers to express concepts in fewer lines of code than would be possible in other languages. At the core of Python's capabilities is the interpreter, which is responsible for executing Python code.

What is a Python Interpreter?

A Python interpreter is a program that reads and executes Python code. It is responsible for translating Python code into machine-readable code that can be executed by the computer's hardware. The interpreter also checks for syntax errors and runs the code line by line. The interpreter plays a vital role in the development of Python applications, as it is responsible for the execution and evaluation of the code.

How does the Python Interpreter Work?

When a Python program is executed, the Python interpreter reads the code line by line and translates it into bytecode, which is a low-level form of code that can be executed by the computer's hardware. The bytecode is then executed by the interpreter, which performs the necessary computations and returns the results to the user. The interpreter also checks for syntax errors, such as missing parentheses or invalid variable names, and reports them to the user.

Why is the Python Interpreter Important?

The Python interpreter is an essential component of the Python language, as it is responsible for executing Python code. The interpreter's ability to execute code line by line makes it easy for developers to debug their code and identify errors. Additionally, the interpreter's ability to translate Python code into bytecode allows Python to be used on a wide variety of hardware platforms, including smartphones, desktop computers, and even supercomputers.

Conclusion

In conclusion, the Python interpreter is a vital component of the Python language. It is responsible for executing Python code, checking for syntax errors, and translating Python code into bytecode. Python's design philosophy emphasizes code readability, and its syntax allows programmers to express concepts in fewer lines of code than would be possible in other languages. With its popularity in software development, data analysis, and scientific computing, Python's interpreter plays a critical role in the success of Python as a language.

Getting Started with Python Scripting Using Visual Code

Python is a high-level programming language that is widely used for general-purpose programming. It is versatile and can be used for a variety of tasks such as web development, data analysis, machine learning, and more. Python is known for its simple syntax, which makes it easy to learn and use. In this article, we will explore how to write and execute the first Python script using Visual Code.

Installing Visual Code

Visual Code is a popular open-source code editor developed by Microsoft. It is free, cross-platform, and supports many programming languages, including Python. To install Visual Code, visit the official website and download the installer for your operating system. Once downloaded, run the installer and follow the prompts to complete the installation.

Setting Up the Python Environment

Before we can start writing Python scripts in Visual Code, we need to set up the Python environment. Visual Code supports multiple Python interpreters, so you can choose the version of Python that best suits your needs. To set up the Python environment, follow these steps:

Open Visual Code and click on the Extensions tab on the left-hand side.

Search for Python in the search bar and click on Install to install the Python extension for Visual Code.

Once installed, click on the Python button on the left-hand side to open the Python Interactive window.

From the Python Interactive window, you can choose the interpreter you want to use. Click on the Select Interpreter button and choose the interpreter you want to use.

Writing the First Python Script

Now that we have set up the Python environment, we can start writing our first Python script. To create a new Python file, follow these steps:

Click on the File menu and select New File.

Type in the code for your Python script. For example, you can print the message "Hello, World!" using the following code:

```
print("Hello, World!")
```

Save the file with a .py extension. For example, you can save the file as hello.py.
Executing the Python Script

To execute the Python script in Visual Code, follow these steps:

Click on the Terminal menu and select New Terminal.

In the terminal window, navigate to the directory where your Python script is saved. For example, if your script is saved in the Documents folder, type the following command:

```
cd Documents
```

Once you are in the correct directory, type the following command to execute the Python script:

```
python hello.py
```

The message "Hello, World!" will be printed in the terminal window.

Python is a widely-used programming language that is known for its simplicity, readability, and flexibility. One of the key features of Python is its core data types, which are the building blocks of any program. In this article, we will explore Python's core data types and their functionality, without using the article word.

Introduction to Python Core Data Types

Python is a dynamically-typed language, which means that the data type of a variable is determined at runtime. This flexibility is possible because Python has several core data types, which can be used to store and manipulate different types of data.

Numeric Data Types

Python supports several numeric data types, including integers, floating-point numbers, and complex numbers. Integers are whole numbers, while floating-point numbers have decimal places. Complex numbers are numbers with a real and imaginary component.

Sequences

Sequences are ordered collections of elements. Python has three main types of sequences: lists, tuples, and ranges. Lists and tuples can contain any type of data, while ranges are used to represent a range of numbers.

Strings

Strings are sequences of characters. They can be created using single or double quotes, and can be manipulated using a variety of methods. In Python, strings are immutable, meaning that once they are created, they cannot be changed.

Sets and Dictionaries

Sets and dictionaries are used to store collections of data that are not ordered. Sets contain unique elements, while dictionaries store key-value pairs.

Converting Between Data Types

Python makes it easy to convert between different data types. For example, you can convert a string to an integer using the int() function, or convert a list to a set using the set() function.

In conclusion, Python's core data types are an essential part of the language's flexibility and ease-of-use. By understanding these data types and their functionality, you can write more efficient and effective code. Whether you are a beginner or an experienced programmer, mastering Python's core data types is a crucial step in becoming a skilled Python developer.

Setting up your Python Environment: A Comprehensive Guide

Python is a powerful programming language that has been gaining popularity over the years, thanks to its simple syntax, powerful libraries, and versatility. Before you can start programming in Python, you need to set up your Python environment. In this comprehensive guide, we will go through the steps required to set up a Python environment on your computer, without using the article word.

Downloading Python

The first step in setting up your Python environment is to download Python from the official website. Choose the appropriate version of Python for your operating system and download the installer.

Installing Python

Once you have downloaded the installer, run it and follow the installation wizard. Make sure to choose the correct options for your installation, such as adding Python to your PATH environment variable.

Choosing a Text Editor or IDE
After installing Python, you will need a text editor or integrated development environment (IDE) to write and run your Python code. There are several options available, such as PyCharm, Visual Studio Code, Sublime Text, and Atom.

Installing a Text Editor or IDE

Download and install your preferred text editor or IDE. Some text editors, such as Sublime Text and Atom, are free, while others, such as PyCharm and Visual Studio Code, have both free and paid versions.

Configuring Your Environment

After installing Python and a text editor or IDE, you will need to configure your environment. This includes setting up your PATH environment variable, installing Python packages, and configuring your text editor or IDE.

Installing Python Packages

Python has a vast collection of third-party packages that you can use to extend its functionality. You can use pip, the Python package manager, to install these packages. To install a package, open your command prompt or terminal and type "pip install package_name".

Virtual Environments

Virtual environments are a way to create isolated Python environments for your projects. They allow you to install packages and manage dependencies without affecting other projects. You can create a virtual environment using the venv module, which is included in Python 3.

Setting up a Virtual Environment

To set up a virtual environment, navigate to your project directory and run "python -m venv env_name" in your command prompt or terminal. This will create a new virtual environment with the name "env_name". Activate your virtual environment by running "source env_name/bin/activate" on macOS or Linux, or "env_name\Scripts\activate" on Windows.

In conclusion, setting up your Python environment is an essential step in starting your Python programming journey. With this guide, you now have a comprehensive understanding of the steps required to set up your Python environment on your computer. With your environment set up, you can now start writing and running Python code, installing packages, and creating virtual environments. Happy coding!

• Python basic syntax and data types

Python is a popular high-level programming language that is widely used for web development, data analysis, artificial intelligence, and more. It is known for its simple syntax, readability, and ease of use. In this article, we will explore the basics of Python syntax and data types, which are essential concepts for any beginner to learn.

Variables and Data Types
In Python, variables are used to store values that can be used throughout the program. To create a variable, you simply need to choose a name for it and assign a value to it using the "=" symbol. For example, to create a variable called "x" and assign it a value of 10, you would write:

x = 10

Python supports several data types, including:

Integers: These are whole numbers, such as 1, 2, 3, and so on.
Floats: These are numbers with decimal points, such as 1.5, 2.7, and so on.
Strings: These are sequences of characters, such as "Hello, world!" or "Python is awesome!".
Booleans: These are either True or False.
To determine the data type of a variable, you can use the type() function. For example, to determine the data type of the variable "x", you would write:

print(type(x))

This would output "int", indicating that "x" is an integer.

Basic Operators
Python supports several basic operators for performing arithmetic and logical operations. These include:

Addition: "+"
Subtraction: "-"
Multiplication: "*"
Division: "/"
Modulus: "%"
Comparison operators: "<", ">", "<=", ">=", "==", "!="
For example, to add two variables "x" and "y", you would write:

z = x + y

This would assign the sum of "x" and "y" to the variable "z". Similarly, to compare two variables "a" and "b", you would write:

```
if a > b:
print("a is greater than b")
else:
print("b is greater than a")
```

This would output either "a is greater than b" or "b is greater than a" depending on the values of "a" and "b".

Conditional Statements
Conditional statements are used to execute certain code only if a certain condition is met. In Python, conditional statements are created using the "if", "else", and "elif" keywords. For example, to check if a variable "x" is greater than 10, you would write:

```
if x > 10:
print("x is greater than 10")
else:
print("x is less than or equal to 10")
```

This would output either "x is greater than 10" or "x is less than or equal to 10" depending on the value of "x".

Loops
Loops are used to execute a block of code repeatedly. In Python, there are two main types of loops: "for" loops and "while" loops. For example, to iterate over a list of numbers and print each one, you would write:

```
numbers = [1, 2, 3, 4, 5]

for num in numbers:
print(num)
```

This would output:

```
1
2
3
4
5
```

Similarly, to execute a block of code while a certain condition is true, you would use a while loop. For example, to print all even numbers between 0 and 10, you would write:

```
i = 0

while i <= 10:
if i % 2 == 0:
print(i)
i += 1
```

This would output:

```
0
2
4
6
8
10
```

Input and Output
Input and output operations are used to communicate with the user or with other parts of the program. In Python, the "input()" function is used to get input from the user, and the "print()" function is used to display output on the screen. For example, to ask the user for their name and print a greeting, you would write:

```
name = input("What is your name? ")
print("Hello, " + name + "!")
```

This would output something like "Hello, John!" if the user entered the name "John".

In addition to printing output to the screen, you can also write data to files using Python's file handling functions. For example, to write a list of numbers to a file called "numbers.txt", you would write:

```
numbers = [1, 2, 3, 4, 5]

with open("numbers.txt", "w") as file:
for num in numbers:
file.write(str(num) + "\n")
```

This would create a file called "numbers.txt" and write the numbers 1 through 5 to it, each on a separate line.

Python syntax and data types are fundamental concepts that every beginner should understand. By mastering variables, data types, operators, conditional statements, loops, and input/output operations, you will be well on your way to writing useful and powerful Python programs. Remember to practice regularly and experiment with different types of programs to gain experience and confidence in your skills.

Variables and Data Types

Variables and data types are essential concepts for any beginner to understand when learning the Python programming language. In this article, we will explore these concepts in detail and provide examples to help you better understand how they work.

What are Variables?

Variables are essentially containers that hold values, such as numbers, text, or objects. These values can then be used throughout a program, making it easier to read, write, and manipulate data. In Python, variables are created simply by assigning a value to a name using the "=" sign. For example, to create a variable called "number" and assign it the value of 5, you would write:

```
number = 5
```

Once a variable has been created, it can be referenced and manipulated throughout the program. For example, you can add two variables together, like so:

```
a = 2
b = 3
c = a + b
```

In this example, we create two variables, "a" and "b", and then create a third variable, "c", that adds the values of "a" and "b" together.

What are Data Types?

Data types are the classification of values that variables can hold. Python supports several different data types, including integers, floats, strings, and booleans. Each data type has its own unique set of properties and operations that can be performed on it.

Integers

Integers are whole numbers, such as 1, 2, 3, and so on. In Python, integers can be represented using the "int" data type. For example, to create a variable called "age" and assign it the value of 25, you would write:

```
age = 25
```

Floats

Floats are numbers with decimal points, such as 1.5, 2.7, and so on. In Python, floats can be represented using the "float" data type. For example, to create a variable called "price" and assign it the value of 4.99, you would write:

price = 4.99

Strings

Strings are sequences of characters, such as "Hello, world!" or "Python is awesome!". In Python, strings can be represented using the "str" data type. For example, to create a variable called "name" and assign it the value of "John Doe", you would write:

name = "John Doe"

Booleans

Booleans are a type of data that can only have one of two values: True or False. In Python, booleans can be represented using the "bool" data type. For example, to create a variable called "is_active" and assign it the value of True, you would write:

is_active = True

Type Conversion

Python also provides the ability to convert between different data types. For example, you can convert a string to an integer using the "int()" function, like so:

```
string_number = "5"
integer_number = int(string_number)
```

In this example, we create a variable called "string_number" and assign it the value of "5" as a string. We then use the "int()" function to convert it to an integer and assign the result to a new variable called "integer_number".

Variables and data types are fundamental concepts in Python that you will use in every program you write. By understanding how to create variables and work with different data types, you will be able to write more complex and powerful programs. Remember to practice regularly and experiment with different types of programs to gain experience and confidence in your skills.

Basic Operators

Basic Operators are essential building blocks of programming in any language, including Python. In this article, we will explore the different types of basic operators in Python and provide examples to help you understand how they work.

Arithmetic Operators

Arithmetic operators are used to perform mathematical operations on numbers in Python. Python supports the following arithmetic operators:

Addition (+)
Subtraction (-)
Multiplication (*)
Division (/)
Modulus (%)
Exponentiation (**)
Here's an example that demonstrates the use of arithmetic operators in Python:

```
a = 5
b = 2
```

Addition
```
print(a + b) # Output: 7
```

Subtraction
```
print(a - b) # Output: 3
```

Multiplication
```
print(a * b) # Output: 10
```

Division
```
print(a / b) # Output: 2.5
```

Modulus
```
print(a % b) # Output: 1
```

Exponentiation
```
print(a ** b) # Output: 25
```

Comparison Operators

Comparison operators are used to compare two values in Python and return a Boolean value (True or False) based on the result of the comparison. Python supports the following comparison operators:

Equal to (==)
Not equal to (!=)
Greater than (>)
Less than (<)
Greater than or equal to (>=)
Less than or equal to (<=)
Here's an example that demonstrates the use of comparison operators in Python:

```
a = 5
b = 3
```

Equal to
print(a == b) # Output: False

Not equal to
print(a != b) # Output: True

Greater than
print(a > b) # Output: True

Less than
print(a < b) # Output: False

Greater than or equal to
print(a >= b) # Output: True

Less than or equal to
print(a <= b) # Output: False

Logical Operators

Logical operators are used to combine Boolean values and return a Boolean value based on the result of the combination. Python supports the following logical operators:

and
or
not

Here's an example that demonstrates the use of logical operators in Python:

```
a = True
b = False
```

and
```
print(a and b) # Output: False
```

or
```
print(a or b) # Output: True
```

not
```
print(not a) # Output: False
```

Assignment Operators

Assignment operators are used to assign values to variables in Python. They combine the assignment operator (=) with an arithmetic, comparison, or logical operator. Here's an example that demonstrates the use of assignment operators in Python:

```
a = 5
b = 2
```

Addition
```
a += b
print(a) # Output: 7
```

Subtraction
```
a -= b
print(a) # Output: 5
```

Multiplication
```
a *= b
print(a) # Output: 10
```

Division
```
a /= b
print(a) # Output: 5.0
```

Modulus
```
a %= b
print(a) # Output: 1.0
```

Exponentiation

```
a **= b
print(a) # Output: 1.0
```

Basic operators are essential building blocks of programming in Python. By understanding how to use arithmetic, comparison, logical, and assignment operators, you will be able to write more complex and powerful programs. Remember to practice regularly and experiment with different types of programs to gain experience and confidence in your skills.

Conditional Statements

Conditional Statements are used in programming to execute specific code only if certain conditions are met. Python provides a variety of conditional statements that allow programmers to create complex programs. In this article, we will explore the different types of conditional statements in Python and provide examples to help you understand how they work.

If Statement

The most basic type of conditional statement in Python is the If statement. The If statement allows you to execute a block of code only if a specific condition is true. Here's an example that demonstrates the use of an If statement in Python:

```
num = 5

if num > 0:
print("Positive number")
```

Output: Positive number

In this example, the If statement checks whether the value of "num" is greater than 0. If the condition is true, the program prints "Positive number" to the console.

If-Else Statement

The If-Else statement allows you to execute one block of code if a condition is true and another block of code if the condition is false. Here's an example that demonstrates the use of an If-Else statement in Python:

```
num = -5

if num > 0:
print("Positive number")
else:
print("Negative number")
```

Output: Negative number

In this example, the If-Else statement checks whether the value of "num" is greater than 0. If the condition is true, the program prints "Positive number" to the console. If the condition is false, the program prints "Negative number" to the console.

If-Elif-Else Statement

The If-Elif-Else statement allows you to execute different blocks of code based on multiple conditions. The Elif keyword stands for "else if" and allows you to check additional conditions after the If statement. Here's an example that demonstrates the use of an If-Elif-Else statement in Python:

```
num = 0

if num > 0:
print("Positive number")
elif num == 0:
print("Zero")
else:
print("Negative number")
```

Output: Zero

In this example, the If-Elif-Else statement checks whether the value of "num" is greater than 0, equal to 0, or less than 0. If the value of "num" is greater than 0, the program prints "Positive number" to the console. If the value of "num" is equal to 0, the program prints "Zero" to the console. If the value of "num" is less than 0, the program prints "Negative number" to the console.

Nested If Statements

Nested If statements allow you to check for multiple conditions within a single If statement. Here's an example that demonstrates the use of nested If statements in Python:

```
num = 10
```

Loops

Loops are an essential concept in programming and are used to execute a block of code repeatedly. Python provides two main types of loops: the For loop and the While loop. In this article, we will explore the different types of loops in Python and provide examples to help you understand how they work.

For Loop

The For loop is used to iterate over a sequence of elements, such as a list or a string. Here's an example that demonstrates the use of a For loop in Python:

```python
fruits = ["apple", "banana", "cherry"]

for fruit in fruits:
print(fruit)
```

Output:
```
apple
banana
cherry
```

In this example, the For loop iterates over each element in the "fruits" list and prints each element to the console.

You can also use the range() function with a For loop to iterate over a range of numbers. Here's an example:

```python
for i in range(1, 5):
print(i)
```

Output:
```
1
2
3
4
```

In this example, the For loop iterates over a range of numbers from 1 to 4 and prints each number to the console.

While Loop

The While loop is used to execute a block of code repeatedly as long as a condition is true. Here's an example that demonstrates the use of a While loop in Python:

```python
i = 1

while i <= 5:
print(i)
i += 1
```

Output:
```
1
2
3
4
5
```

In this example, the While loop executes the block of code as long as the value of "i" is less than or equal to 5. The program prints the value of "i" to the console and increments the value of "i" by 1 in each iteration of the loop.

You can also use the break and continue statements with a While loop. The break statement is used to exit the loop prematurely, while the continue statement is used to skip over an iteration of the loop. Here's an example:

```python
i = 1

while i <= 10:
if i == 5:
break
if i % 2 == 0:
i += 1
continue
print(i)
i += 1
```

Output:
```
1
3
```

In this example, the While loop executes the block of code as long as the value of "i" is less than or equal to 10. However, the break statement is used to exit the loop prematurely when the value of "i" is equal to 5. The continue statement is used to skip over the iteration of the loop when the value of "i" is even. The program prints the value of "i" to the console for odd numbers only.

Loops are an important concept in programming, and Python provides two main types of loops: the For loop and the While loop. By understanding how to use For and While loops in Python, you can create more complex programs that can iterate over a sequence of elements or execute a block of code repeatedly as long as a certain condition is true.

Input and Output

Python provides built-in functions for input and output operations, which are essential for interacting with users and reading/writing data to files. In this article, we will explore the different ways to perform input and output operations in Python with examples.

Input Operations

The input() function in Python is used to read input from the user. It prompts the user to enter input, reads the input from the console, and returns the value as a string. Here's an example that demonstrates the use of the input() function in Python:

```
name = input("Enter your name: ")
print("Hello, " + name)
```

Output:
Enter your name: John
Hello, John

In this example, the input() function prompts the user to enter their name. The user enters their name "John", which is then stored in the variable "name". The program then uses the value of "name" to print a personalized greeting to the user.

Output Operations

The print() function in Python is used to display output to the console. It takes one or more arguments and prints them to the console. Here's an example that demonstrates the use of the print() function in Python:

```
print("Hello, World!")
```

Output:
Hello, World!

In this example, the print() function takes a string argument "Hello, World!" and prints it to the console.

Reading from and Writing to Files

Python provides built-in functions to read from and write to files. The open() function is used to open a file, and the read() and write() functions are used to read from and write to the file, respectively. Here's an example that demonstrates the use of these functions in Python:

```
Writing to a file
with open("example.txt", "w") as f:
f.write("Hello, World!")
```

```
Reading from a file
with open("example.txt", "r") as f:
contents = f.read()
print(contents)
```

```
Output:
Hello, World!
```

In this example, the with statement is used to open the file "example.txt" in write mode and write the string "Hello, World!" to the file. The same file is then opened in read mode using the with statement, and the contents of the file are read using the read() function. The contents are then printed to the console.

Formatted Output

Python provides several ways to format output using placeholders and formatting strings. Here's an example that demonstrates the use of formatted output in Python:

```
name = "John"
age = 30
```

```
Using placeholders
print("My name is {} and I am {} years old.".format(name, age))
```

```
Using f-strings
print(f"My name is {name} and I am {age} years old.")
```

```
Output:
My name is John and I am 30 years old.
My name is John and I am 30 years old.
```

In this example, the placeholders "{}" are used to format the output string with the values of the variables "name" and "age". The same output can also be achieved using f-strings, which allow you to embed expressions inside string literals using curly braces.

Input and output operations are an essential part of programming, and Python provides built-in functions to perform these operations efficiently. By understanding how to use the input(), print(), open(), read(), and write() functions, as well as formatted output, you can create more complex programs that can read input from users, write output to files, and display formatted output to the console.

```python
if num > 0:
if num % 2 == 0:
print("Positive even number")
else:
print("Positive odd number")
else:
print("Negative number")
```

Output: Positive even number

In this example, the nested If statements first check whether the value of "num" is greater than 0. If the value of "num" is greater than 0, the program checks whether the value of "num" is even or odd. If the value of "num" is even, the program prints "Positive even number" to the console. If the value of "num" is odd, the program prints "Positive odd number" to the console. If the value of "num" is less than or equal to 0, the program prints "Negative number" to the console.

Control structures: if/else, for/while loops

Control structures are an essential part of programming that enable us to control the flow of execution in our code. In Python, the two main control structures are if/else statements and for/while loops. In this article, we will explore these control structures and demonstrate how they can be used in Python.

If/Else Statements

If/else statements allow us to execute different blocks of code based on certain conditions. In Python, if/else statements have the following syntax:

```
if condition:
# block of code to execute if condition is true
else:
# block of code to execute if condition is false
```

Here's an example that demonstrates the use of if/else statements in Python:

```
age = 25

if age >= 18:
print("You are an adult")
else:
print("You are not an adult")
```

Output:
You are an adult

In this example, the if/else statement checks if the value of "age" is greater than or equal to 18. Since the value of "age" is 25, the condition is true and the program prints "You are an adult" to the console.

For Loops

For loops are used to iterate over a sequence of values, such as a list or a tuple. In Python, for loops have the following syntax:

```
for variable in sequence:
# block of code to execute for each value in sequence
```

Here's an example that demonstrates the use of for loops in Python:

```
fruits = ["apple", "banana", "cherry"]

for fruit in fruits:
print(fruit)
```

Output:
apple
banana
cherry

In this example, the for loop iterates over the list of fruits and prints each fruit to the console.

While Loops

While loops are used to execute a block of code repeatedly as long as a certain condition is true. In Python, while loops have the following syntax:

```
while condition:
# block of code to execute while condition is true
```

Here's an example that demonstrates the use of while loops in Python:

```
i = 0

while i < 5:
print(i)
i += 1
```

Output:
0
1
2
3
4

In this example, the while loop executes the block of code as long as the value of "i" is less than 5. The value of "i" is initially 0, and it is incremented by 1 after each iteration of the loop.

Nested Control Structures

It is also possible to use nested control structures in Python, such as an if statement inside a for loop or a while loop inside an if statement. Here's an example that demonstrates a nested control structure in Python:

```
numbers = [1, 2, 3, 4, 5]

for number in numbers:
if number % 2 == 0:
print(f"{number} is even")
else:
print(f"{number} is odd")
```

Output:
1 is odd
2 is even
3 is odd
4 is even
5 is odd

In this example, the for loop iterates over the list of numbers and checks if each number is even or odd using an if statement. The program then prints a message to the console indicating whether the number is even or odd.

Control structures are an essential part of programming that enable us to control the flow of execution in our code. By understanding how to use if/else statements, for loops, and while loops, as well as nested control structures, you can create more complex programs that can perform a wide variety of tasks.

Functions and Modules: A Comprehensive Guide to Python Programming

Functions and modules are fundamental concepts in Python programming. They allow you to organize your code, make it more reusable, and improve its overall structure. In this guide, we will explore the world of functions and modules in Python, covering everything from the basics of defining and calling functions to creating and using packages.

Part 1: Introduction to Functions in Python

Functions are reusable pieces of code that perform a specific task. They can take inputs and return outputs, making them incredibly versatile. In Python, you can define a function using the "def" keyword followed by the function name, input arguments, and the code that defines what the function does. Here is an example:

```
def add_numbers(x, y):
    return x + y
```

In this example, we defined a function called "add_numbers" that takes two input arguments, "x" and "y". The function then returns the sum of "x" and "y". To call this function, we can simply pass two values to it, like this:

```
result = add_numbers(3, 5)
print(result)
```

This would output "8", which is the sum of 3 and 5.

Part 2: Working with Modules in Python

Modules are files containing Python code that can be imported into other Python code. They allow you to reuse code across multiple programs and make your code more organized. Python comes with many built-in modules, such as "math" and "random", which provide functions for mathematical calculations and generating random numbers, respectively.

To use a module in your code, you need to import it first. You can do this using the "import" keyword, followed by the name of the module. Here is an example:

```
import math

result = math.sqrt(25)
print(result)
```

In this example, we imported the "math" module and used its "sqrt" function to calculate the square root of 25. This would output "5.0".

Part 3: Advanced Function Concepts in Python

Python functions can be quite powerful, and there are many advanced concepts that you can use to make them even more versatile. Some of these concepts include default arguments, variable-length argument lists, and recursion.

Default arguments allow you to define a default value for an input argument, which is used if no value is provided when the function is called. Here is an example:

```python
def greet(name="World"):
    print("Hello, " + name + "!")

greet("Alice")
greet()
```

In this example, we defined a function called "greet" that takes a default argument of "World" for the "name" input. When we call the function with the argument "Alice", it outputs "Hello, Alice!". When we call the function without an argument, it uses the default value and outputs "Hello, World!".

Variable-length argument lists allow you to define a function that can take a variable number of input arguments. Here is an example:

```python
def sum_numbers(*args):
    result = 0
    for num in args:
        result += num
    return result

print(sum_numbers(1, 2, 3))
print(sum_numbers(4, 5, 6, 7))
```

In this example, we defined a function called "sum_numbers" that takes a variable-length argument list using the "*" operator. The function then iterates over the input arguments and returns their sum. When we call the function with the arguments 1, 2, and 3, it outputs "6". When we call the function with the arguments 4, 5, 6, and 7, it outputs "22".

Recursion is a technique where a function calls itself. This can be useful for solving problems that can be broken down into smaller subproblems. Here is an example:

```
def factorial(n):
    if n == 0:
        return 1
    else:
        return n * factorial(n-1)

print(factorial(5))
```

In this example, we defined a function called "factorial" that calculates the factorial of a number using recursion. The base case of the recursion is when "n" is equal to 0, in which case the function returns 1. Otherwise, the function multiplies "n" by the result of calling "factorial" with "n-1". When we call the function with the argument 5, it outputs "120", which is the factorial of 5.

Part 4: Creating and Using Packages in Python

Packages are collections of modules that can be used to organize your code and create reusable libraries. To create a package in Python, you need to create a directory with a special file called "init.py". This file tells Python that the directory is a package and can contain other modules.

Here is an example of how to create a simple package:

Create a new directory called "my_package".
Create a file called "init.py" inside the "my_package" directory.
Create a file called "my_module.py" inside the "my_package" directory.
Add some code to the "my_module.py" file, such as a function that adds two numbers.
Import the package and module in your Python code and use the function.
Here is an example:

```
# Inside my_module.py
def add_numbers(x, y):
    return x + y

# Inside your Python code
import my_package.my_module

result = my_package.my_module.add_numbers(3, 5)
print(result)
```

In this example, we created a package called "my_package" that contains a module called "my_module". The "my_module" module contains a function called "add_numbers" that adds two numbers. We then imported the package and module into our Python code and used the "add_numbers" function to add 3 and 5, which outputs "8".

Part 5: Best Practices for Functions and Modules in Python

When writing functions and modules in Python, it is important to follow best practices to ensure that your code is easy to read, maintain, and reuse. Some best practices include:

Writing modular and reusable code
Using descriptive variable and function names
Writing docstrings for your code
Using proper indentation and whitespace
Following naming conventions, such as using lowercase names for functions and modules
By following these best practices, you can create high-quality Python code that is easy to understand and use.

Functions and modules are essential concepts in Python programming. They allow you to organize your code, make it more reusable, and improve its overall structure. By understanding the basics of defining and calling functions, importing and using modules, and using advanced function concepts, you can create powerful Python programs. Additionally, by creating and using packages and following best practices for functions and modules, you can make your code more organized, maintainable, and reusable.

Input/Output in Python

Part 1: Introduction to Input/Output in Python

Input and output (I/O) are important concepts in programming. In Python, you can use various functions to read and write data from and to different sources, such as files, the console, or the network. I/O operations are critical for building applications that interact with users, data storage, or other systems.

Part 2: Reading Data from Files in Python

Reading data from files is a common task in Python. You can read data from various file formats, such as text, CSV, JSON, or binary files. Python provides several built-in functions to read data from files, such as "open()" and "read()".

Here is an example of how to read data from a text file:

```
file = open("data.txt", "r")
content = file.read()
file.close()

print(content)
```

In this example, we first open a file called "data.txt" in read mode ("r"). We then read the content of the file using the "read()" function and store it in a variable called "content". Finally, we close the file using the "close()" function and print the content.

Part 3: Writing Data to Files in Python

Writing data to files is also a common task in Python. You can write data to various file formats, such as text, CSV, JSON, or binary files. Python provides several built-in functions to write data to files, such as "open()" and "write()".

Here is an example of how to write data to a text file:

```
file = open("data.txt", "w")
file.write("Hello, world!")
file.close()
```

In this example, we first open a file called "data.txt" in write mode ("w"). We then write the string "Hello, world!" to the file using the "write()" function. Finally, we close the file using the "close()" function.

Part 4: Reading and Writing CSV Files in Python

CSV (comma-separated values) files are a common file format for storing and exchanging tabular data. In Python, you can use the "csv" module to read and write CSV files. This module provides various functions and classes to handle CSV files, such as "csv.reader()", "csv.writer()", and "csv.DictReader()".

Here is an example of how to read a CSV file using the "csv" module:

```
import csv

with open("data.csv", "r") as file:
    reader = csv.reader(file)
    for row in reader:
        print(row)
```

In this example, we first import the "csv" module. We then open a file called "data.csv" in read mode using a "with" statement, which automatically closes the file after we're done reading it. We then create a reader object using the "csv.reader()" function and loop over the rows in the file using a "for" loop. Finally, we print each row to the console.

Here is an example of how to write a CSV file using the "csv" module:

```
import csv

data = [
    ["Name", "Age", "City"],
    ["John", "25", "New York"],
    ["Jane", "30", "San Francisco"],
    ["Bob", "35", "Chicago"],
]

with open("data.csv", "w", newline="") as file:
    writer = csv.writer(file)
    writer.writerows(data)
```

In this example, we first import the "csv" module. We then define a list of lists called "data", where each inner list represents a row in the CSV file. We then open a file called "data.csv" in write mode using a "with" statement and specify the "newline" parameter to prevent the writer from inserting additional line breaks. We then create a writer object using the "csv.writer()" function and use the "writerows()" method to write the data to the file.

Part 5: Reading and Writing JSON Files in Python

JSON (JavaScript Object Notation) is a lightweight data interchange format that is easy for humans to read and write and easy for machines to parse and generate. In Python, you can use the "json" module to read and write JSON files. This module provides various functions and classes to handle JSON files, such as "json.load()", "json.loads()", "json.dump()", and "json.dumps()".

Here is an example of how to read a JSON file using the "json" module:

```python
import json

with open("data.json", "r") as file:
    data = json.load(file)

print(data)
```

In this example, we first import the "json" module. We then open a file called "data.json" in read mode using a "with" statement, which automatically closes the file after we're done reading it. We then use the "json.load()" function to parse the JSON data from the file and store it in a variable called "data". Finally, we print the "data" variable to the console.

Here is an example of how to write a JSON file using the "json" module:

```python
import json

data = {
    "name": "John",
    "age": 25,
    "city": "New York"
}

with open("data.json", "w") as file:
    json.dump(data, file)
```

In this example, we first import the "json" module. We then define a dictionary called "data" that contains some data to be written to the JSON file. We then open a file called "data.json" in write mode using a "with" statement and create a JSON encoder using the "json.dump()" function. We then use the "dump()" method to encode the data as JSON and write it to the file.

Part 6: Reading and Writing Binary Files in Python

Binary files are files that contain data in a binary format, which is different from the text-based formats we've seen so far. Binary files can contain any type of data, such as images, audio, video, or serialized objects. In Python, you can use the "open()" function with the "rb" and "wb" modes to read and write binary files.

Here is an example of how to read a binary file in Python:

```
with open("data.bin", "rb") as file:
    data = file.read()

print(data)
```

In this example, we open a file called "data.bin" in read mode with the "rb" mode. We then read the contents of the file using the "read()" method and store it in a variable called "data". Finally, we print the "data" variable to the console.

Here is an example of how to write a binary file in Python:

```
data = b'\x00\x01\x02\x03\x04'

with open("data.bin", "wb") as file:
    file.write(data)
```

In this example, we define a bytes object called "data" that contains some binary data to be written to the file. We then open a file called "data.bin" in write mode with the "wb" mode and write the "data" object to the file using the "write()" method.

Working with files

Part 1: Introduction

Working with files is an essential part of programming, and Python provides various functions and modules to handle file operations. In this article, we'll explore the different ways of working with files in Python and see some code examples.

Part 2: Opening and Closing Files in Python

Before we can work with a file in Python, we need to open it using the "open()" function. The "open()" function takes two arguments: the filename and the mode in which to open the file. The mode can be "r" for reading, "w" for writing, "a" for appending, "x" for exclusive creation, "b" for binary mode, and "t" for text mode.

Here is an example of how to open a file for reading:

```
file = open("data.txt", "r")
```

In this example, we open a file called "data.txt" in read mode and store the file object in a variable called "file". Once we're done working with the file, we need to close it using the "close()" method:

```
file.close()
```

This method ensures that any changes made to the file are saved, and any resources used by the file are freed.

Part 3: Reading Files in Python

Once we've opened a file for reading, we can read its contents using various methods provided by Python. Here is an example of how to read the entire contents of a file:

```
with open("data.txt", "r") as file:
    data = file.read()

print(data)
```

In this example, we open a file called "data.txt" in read mode using a "with" statement, which automatically closes the file after we're done reading it. We then use the "read()" method to read the entire contents of the file and store it in a variable called "data". Finally, we print the "data" variable to the console.

Here is an example of how to read a file line by line:

```
with open("data.txt", "r") as file:
    for line in file:
        print(line)
```

In this example, we open a file called "data.txt" in read mode using a "with" statement, which automatically closes the file after we're done reading it. We then use a "for" loop to iterate over the file object and print each line to the console.

Part 4: Writing Files in Python

Once we've opened a file for writing, we can write data to it using various methods provided by Python. Here is an example of how to write a string to a file:

```
with open("data.txt", "w") as file:
    file.write("Hello, world!")
```

In this example, we open a file called "data.txt" in write mode using a "with" statement, which automatically closes the file after we're done writing to it. We then use the "write()" method to write the string "Hello, world!" to the file.

Here is an example of how to write a list of strings to a file:

```
data = ["apple", "banana", "orange"]

with open("data.txt", "w") as file:
    for item in data:
        file.write(item + "\n")
```

In this example, we define a list of strings called "data" that we want to write to a file. We then open a file called "data.txt" in write mode using a "with" statement, which automatically closes the file after we're done writing to it. We then use a "for" loop to iterate over the list of strings and write each item to the file,separating them by a new line character ("\n").

Part 5: Appending to Files in Python

If we want to add new data to an existing file, we can open the file in "append" mode using the "a" argument. Here is an example of how to append a string to a file:

```
with open("data.txt", "a") as file:
    file.write("This is a new line!")
```

In this example, we open a file called "data.txt" in append mode using a "with" statement, which automatically closes the file after we're done appending to it. We then use the "write()" method to append the string "This is a new line!" to the file.

Part 6: Working with Binary Files in Python

In addition to working with text files, Python can also handle binary files such as images, videos, and audio files. Here is an example of how to read the contents of a binary file:

```
with open("image.jpg", "rb") as file:
    data = file.read()

print(data)
```

In this example, we open a file called "image.jpg" in binary mode using a "with" statement, which automatically closes the file after we're done reading it. We then use the "read()" method to read the entire contents of the file and store it in a variable called "data". Finally, we print the "data" variable to the console.

Part 7: Working with Files in Different Directories

By default, Python looks for files in the same directory as the script that's running. However, we can also specify the path to a file to work with files in different directories. Here is an example of how to open a file in a different directory:

```
with open("/path/to/file/data.txt", "r") as file:
    data = file.read()

print(data)
```

In this example, we specify the path to the file as "/path/to/file/data.txt" and open it in read mode using a "with" statement. We then use the "read()" method to read the entire contents of the file and store it in a variable called "data". Finally, we print the "data" variable to the console.

we explored the different ways of working with files in Python, including opening and closing files, reading and writing data, and working with binary files. We also saw some code examples that illustrate how to work with files in Python. With these concepts and techniques, you can easily handle file operations in your Python programs.

Working with files

Python is a popular programming language used for various purposes such as web development, data analysis, and machine learning. One of the essential aspects of programming is working with files. Files are used to store and retrieve data, and Python provides numerous ways to interact with them. In this article, we will explore various methods to work with files in Python.

Opening and Closing Files:
Before we can work with a file, we need to open it. In Python, we can use the open() function to open a file. The function takes two parameters: the path to the file and the mode in which we want to open it. Modes can be 'r' for reading, 'w' for writing, and 'a' for appending to an existing file. Once we are done with the file, we need to close it using the close() function. Failing to close a file can result in memory leaks and data corruption.

Reading Files:

Python provides several ways to read data from a file. One of the most common methods is to read the entire file using the read() function. The function returns a string containing the contents of the file. Another way is to read the file line by line using the readline() function. The function reads a single line from the file and returns it as a string. We can also use the readlines() function to read all the lines of the file and return them as a list of strings.

Writing to Files:
To write data to a file, we need to open the file in 'w' or 'a' mode. 'w' mode overwrites the existing file, while 'a' mode appends to an existing file. We can write to a file using the write() function, which takes a string as a parameter. We can also write multiple lines of data using the writelines() function, which takes a list of strings as a parameter.

Closing Files:

As mentioned earlier, we need to close a file after we are done working with it. In Python, we can use the with statement to automatically close a file after we are done with it. The with statement ensures that the file is closed even if an error occurs. Here's an example:

```
with open('example.txt', 'r') as file:
    # Perform operations on the file
```

Working with Binary Files:
In addition to text files, we can also work with binary files in Python. Binary files contain non-textual data such as images, audio, and video. To read and write binary files, we need to open them in binary mode using the 'b' character in the mode parameter. Here's an example of opening a binary file:

```
with open('example.bin', 'rb') as file:
    # Perform operations on the binary file
```

Working with files is an essential aspect of programming, and Python provides various methods to interact with them. We can read and write text files, as well as binary files. It's crucial to remember to close files after we are done working with them to avoid memory leaks and data corruption. The with statement can be used to automatically close files and ensure that they are closed even if an error occurs.

Error handling in Python

Error handling is a critical aspect of programming. As programmers, we can never assume that everything will always go as planned. Python provides several ways to handle errors in our code. In this article, we will explore different error handling techniques in Python.

What is an Error?

In programming, an error is a deviation from the expected behavior of a program. Errors can be classified into two types: syntax errors and runtime errors. Syntax errors occur when the code violates the rules of the language. Runtime errors occur when the code is syntactically correct but encounters an issue during execution.

Types of Errors:

There are several types of errors in Python, such as NameError, TypeError, ValueError, ZeroDivisionError, and ImportError. Each error type indicates a specific problem in the code. For example, NameError occurs when we try to use a variable that has not been defined, while TypeError occurs when we try to perform an operation on incompatible types.

Try and Except Blocks:
Python provides a built-in exception handling mechanism using the try and except blocks. We can use the try block to wrap the code that might raise an exception. If an exception occurs, the except block is executed. Here's an example:

```
try:
    # Code that might raise an exception
except ExceptionType:
    # Code to handle the exception
```

In this example, ExceptionType is the type of exception we want to handle. We can also use a bare except block to catch all types of exceptions. However, it's generally not a good practice as it can mask other issues in the code.

Raising Exceptions:

We can also raise our own exceptions using the raise statement. We can raise exceptions for specific conditions in our code. Here's an example:

```
if x < 0:
    raise ValueError("x cannot be negative")
```

In this example, we raise a ValueError if x is negative. We can also create our own custom exception classes by subclassing the built-in Exception class.

Finally Block:
In addition to the try and except blocks, Python also provides a finally block. The code in the finally block is always executed, regardless of whether an exception occurs or not. Here's an example:

```
try:
    # Code that might raise an exception
except ExceptionType:
    # Code to handle the exception
finally:
    # Code that is always executed
```

Error handling is a crucial aspect of programming, and Python provides several ways to handle errors in our code. We can use the try and except blocks to catch and handle exceptions, raise our own exceptions using the raise statement, and use the finally block to ensure that code is always executed, regardless of exceptions. By using these error handling techniques, we can make our code more robust and reliable.

Object-Oriented Programming (OOP) in Python

Object-Oriented Programming (OOP) is a programming paradigm that focuses on creating objects that encapsulate data and behavior. OOP enables programmers to write code that is more modular, extensible, and reusable. Python is an object-oriented language that supports OOP principles. In this article, we will explore the fundamentals of OOP in Python.

Classes and Objects:
In Python, a class is a blueprint for creating objects. It defines the attributes and methods that an object of that class will have. An object is an instance of a class. We can create multiple objects from the same class, each with its own unique data.

```
class MyClass:
    def __init__(self, arg1, arg2):
        self.arg1 = arg1
        self.arg2 = arg2

obj1 = MyClass(1, 2)
obj2 = MyClass(3, 4)
```

In this example, we define a MyClass class with two attributes arg1 and arg2. We then create two objects obj1 and obj2 from the MyClass class, passing in different arguments to their constructors.

Inheritance:

Inheritance is a mechanism by which one class can inherit attributes and methods from another class. The class that inherits from another class is called a subclass or derived class, and the class that is inherited from is called the superclass or base class.

```
class MySubClass(MyClass):
    def my_method(self):
        # Code that uses inherited attributes and methods
```

In this example, we define a MySubClass subclass that inherits from the MyClass superclass. The MySubClass subclass can use the attributes and methods of the MyClass superclass, in addition to defining its own unique attributes and methods.

Polymorphism:

Polymorphism is the ability of objects to take on different forms. In Python, polymorphism can be achieved through method overriding and method overloading. Method overriding is when a subclass redefines a method that is already defined in the superclass. Method overloading is when a class has multiple methods with the same name but different arguments.

```
class MySubClass(MyClass):
    def my_method(self):
        # Override the superclass method

    def my_method(self, arg1):
        # Overload the method with a different number of arguments
```

In this example, we define a MySubClass subclass that overrides the my_method method defined in the MyClass superclass. We also define an overloaded version of my_method that takes in an additional argument.

Encapsulation:

Encapsulation is the practice of hiding the internal details of an object from the outside world. In Python, encapsulation can be achieved through the use of private attributes and methods.

```
class MyClass:
    def __init__(self):
        self._my_private_attr = 1

    def my_public_method(self):
        # Code that uses the private attribute
```

In this example, we define a MyClass class with a private attribute _my_private_attr. The attribute is marked as private by prefixing it with an underscore. The class also has a public method my_public_method that can access the private attribute.

Object-Oriented Programming is a powerful paradigm that can make our code more modular, extensible, and reusable. In Python, we can use classes and objects to encapsulate data and behavior, inherit attributes and methods from other classes, achieve polymorphism through method overriding and overloading, and encapsulate our objects' internal details using private attributes and methods. By using these OOP principles, we can write code that is easier to maintain and more robust.

Inheritance and polymorphism

Inheritance and polymorphism are two core concepts of Object-Oriented Programming (OOP) that allow us to write more efficient and reusable code. In Python, these concepts are fundamental and powerful tools that allow developers to create complex software with ease. In this article, we will explore the basics of inheritance and polymorphism in Python and provide some examples to illustrate their usage.

Inheritance:

Inheritance is a mechanism in OOP that allows us to create a new class by deriving properties and characteristics from an existing class. The existing class is called the base class or the superclass, and the new class is called the derived class or the subclass.

```python
class Animal:
    def __init__(self, name, age):
        self.name = name
        self.age = age

class Dog(Animal):
    def bark(self):
        print("Woof!")
```

In this example, we have defined two classes: Animal and Dog. The Dog class is a subclass of the Animal class, and it inherits the name and age attributes from the Animal class. The Dog class also has a unique method called bark, which is not present in the Animal class.

Polymorphism:

Polymorphism is another essential concept in OOP, which means that objects of different classes can be treated as if they were objects of the same class. It allows us to write more generic and flexible code that can work with different types of objects.class Animal:

```python
class Animal:
    def __init__(self, name, age):
        self.name = name
        self.age = age

    def make_sound(self):
        pass

class Dog(Animal):
    def make_sound(self):
```

```
    print("Woof!")

class Cat(Animal):
    def make_sound(self):
        print("Meow!")
```

In this example, we have defined three classes: Animal, Dog, and Cat. All three classes have a method called make_sound, but the implementation of the method is different in each class. The Animal class has a blank implementation of the make_sound method, while the Dog and Cat classes override the method and implement their own unique behavior.

Inheritance and Polymorphism Combined:

Inheritance and polymorphism can be combined to create more complex and powerful software systems. The derived classes can inherit properties and methods from their base classes, and they can also override and implement their own unique behavior.

```
class Vehicle:
    def __init__(self, name, model):
        self.name = name
        self.model = model

    def drive(self):
        print("Driving...")

class Car(Vehicle):
    def __init__(self, name, model, num_doors):
        super().__init__(name, model)
        self.num_doors = num_doors

    def drive(self):
        print("Driving car...")

class Truck(Vehicle):
    def __init__(self, name, model, payload_capacity):
        super().__init__(name, model)
        self.payload_capacity = payload_capacity

    def drive(self):
        print("Driving truck...")

vehicles = [Car("Honda", "Civic", 4), Truck("Ford", "F-150", 2000)]

for vehicle in vehicles:
    vehicle.drive()
```

Learn Python From an Expert

In this example, we have defined a Vehicle class that has a drive method. We then defined two derived classes: Car and Truck, which inherit from the Vehicle class and override the drive method with their unique implementations. We create a list of Car and Truck objects and call the drive method on each object.

Regular expressions in Python

Regular expressions are a powerful tool for pattern matching and text manipulation in Python. Whether you're parsing a large dataset or searching for specific strings in a document, regular expressions can help you get the job done quickly and efficiently.

What are Regular Expressions?

At their core, regular expressions are a way to describe patterns in text. They allow you to search for specific sequences of characters, such as all words that start with "cat" or all phone numbers formatted in a certain way.

Regular expressions use a combination of metacharacters and literal characters to define the patterns you're searching for. For example, the "." metacharacter matches any single character, while the "*" metacharacter matches zero or more occurrences of the preceding character.

Using Regular Expressions in Python

Python provides a built-in module for regular expressions called "re". This module provides a number of functions for working with regular expressions, including searching for patterns, replacing patterns, and splitting text based on patterns.

To use regular expressions in Python, you first need to import the "re" module:

```
import re
```

Searching for Patterns

One of the most common uses of regular expressions is searching for patterns in text. The "re.search()" function allows you to search for a pattern in a string and return the first match:

Searching for Patterns

One of the most common uses of regular expressions is searching for patterns in text. The "re.search()" function allows you to search for a pattern in a string and return the first match:

In this example, we're searching for the word "brown" in the string "The quick brown fox jumps over the lazy dog". The "re.search()" function returns a match object, which we can use to get the matched text using the "group()" method.

Replacing Patterns

Another useful feature of regular expressions is the ability to replace patterns in text. The "re.sub()" function allows you to search for a pattern and replace it with a new string:

```python
text = "The quick brown fox jumps over the lazy dog"
pattern = "brown"

new_text = re.sub(pattern, "red", text)
print(new_text)
```

In this example, we're searching for the word "brown" and replacing it with the word "red". The "re.sub()" function returns a new string with the pattern replaced.

Splitting Text

Regular expressions can also be used to split text based on patterns. The "re.split()" function allows you to split a string into a list of substrings based on a pattern:

```python
text = "The quick brown fox jumps over the lazy dog"
pattern = "\s+" # split on one or more whitespace characters

substrings = re.split(pattern, text)
print(substrings)
```

In this example, we're splitting the string based on one or more whitespace characters. The "re.split()" function returns a list of substrings.

Regular expressions are a powerful tool for pattern matching and text manipulation in Python. They allow you to search for specific patterns in text, replace patterns with new strings, and split text into substrings based on patterns. By learning how to use regular expressions in Python, you can greatly enhance your text processing capabilities.

Lambda functions and functional programming

Lambda functions and functional programming are powerful tools in Python for creating concise and efficient code. With lambda functions, you can write simple functions on the fly without defining them beforehand. In this article, we will explore the concept of lambda functions and how they are used in functional programming.

Introduction to Lambda Functions

Lambda functions, also known as anonymous functions, are functions that are not bound to a name. They are defined using the lambda keyword and can take any number of arguments. Lambda functions are commonly used in functional programming to create short and simple functions.

Here is an example of a lambda function:

```
lambda x, y: x + y
```

This lambda function takes two arguments, x and y, and returns their sum. The function can be assigned to a variable and used like any other function:

```
add = lambda x, y: x + y
result = add(3, 4)
print(result) # Output: 7
```

Using Lambda Functions in Functional Programming

Functional programming is a programming paradigm that emphasizes the use of functions to create reusable code. Lambda functions are a key tool in functional programming because they allow you to create small, reusable functions on the fly.

In functional programming, lambda functions are often used with higher-order functions, which are functions that take other functions as arguments. For example, the built-in map() function in Python takes a function and applies it to every element in a sequence. Here is an example of using a lambda function with the map() function:

```
numbers = [1, 2, 3, 4, 5]
squares = map(lambda x: x ** 2, numbers)
print(list(squares)) # Output: [1, 4, 9, 16, 25]
```

In this example, we define a lambda function that takes a number and returns its square. We then use the map() function to apply the lambda function to every element in the numbers list.

Lambda functions can also be used with filter() function in Python, which filters elements from a sequence based on a condition:

```
numbers = [1, 2, 3, 4, 5, 6, 7, 8, 9, 10]
even_numbers = filter(lambda x: x % 2 == 0, numbers)
print(list(even_numbers)) # Output: [2, 4, 6, 8, 10]

numbers = [1, 2, 3, 4, 5, 6, 7, 8, 9, 10]
even_numbers = filter(lambda x: x % 2 == 0, numbers)
print(list(even_numbers)) # Output: [2, 4, 6, 8, 10]
```

In this example, we define a lambda function that takes a number and returns True if it's even. We then use the filter() function to apply the lambda function to every element in the numbers list and return only the even numbers.

Advantages of Lambda Functions

Lambda functions offer several advantages over traditional functions. First, they are concise and easy to read, which makes them ideal for simple, one-time functions. Second, they can be used in functional programming to create reusable code. Finally, lambda functions are often used in conjunction with higher-order functions, which can lead to more efficient and readable code.

Lambda functions are a powerful tool in Python for creating concise and efficient code. They are commonly used in functional programming to create small, reusable functions on the fly. By learning how to use lambda functions, you can greatly enhance your programming skills and create more efficient and readable code.

Decorators

Decorators are a powerful feature in Python that allow you to modify the behavior of a function or class without modifying its source code. They provide a clean and efficient way to add functionality to your code and make it more readable and maintainable.

Introduction to Decorators

Decorators are functions that take another function as input and return a new function as output. They are used to modify the behavior of the input function, without changing its original code. Decorators are commonly used to add functionality such as caching, logging, authentication, and performance monitoring to a function or class.

Here is an example of a decorator that adds logging functionality to a function:

```python
def log_decorator(func):
    def wrapper(*args, **kwargs):
        print(f"Calling function {func.__name__}")
        result = func(*args, **kwargs)
        print(f"Finished calling function {func.__name__}")
        return result
    return wrapper

@log_decorator
def add(x, y):
    return x + y
```

In this example, the log_decorator function is a decorator that takes a function as input and returns a new function that adds logging functionality to the original function. The wrapper function is the new function that is returned by the decorator. It takes any number of positional and keyword arguments and passes them to the original function. The result variable stores the return value of the original function, which is then returned by the wrapper function.

Using Decorators in Python

Decorators are used in Python to add functionality to functions or classes. You can use them to add features such as caching, logging, performance monitoring, and authentication to your code. Here is an example of using a decorator to add caching functionality to a function:

```python
def cache_decorator(func):
    cache = {}
    def wrapper(*args):
        if args in cache:
```

```
        return cache[args]
    result = func(*args)
    cache[args] = result
    return result
return wrapper

@cache_decorator
def fib(n):
    if n <= 1:
        return n
    return fib(n-1) + fib(n-2)
```

In this example, the cache_decorator function is a decorator that takes a function as input and returns a new function that adds caching functionality to the original function. The cache variable stores a cache of previously computed results. The wrapper function first checks if the result for the given arguments is already in the cache. If it is, it returns the cached result. Otherwise, it computes the result using the original function and stores it in the cache.

Benefits of Decorators

Decorators offer several benefits in Python. First, they allow you to add functionality to a function or class without modifying its original code, which makes your code more maintainable and reusable. Second, they allow you to separate concerns and keep your code organized by grouping related functionality together in decorators. Finally, they allow you to create clean and efficient code by eliminating the need for redundant code.

Decorators are a powerful feature in Python that allow you to modify the behavior of a function or class without changing its original code. They provide a clean and efficient way to add functionality to your code and make it more readable and maintainable. By learning how to use decorators, you can greatly enhance your programming skills and create more efficient and reusable code.

Generators and iterators

Generators and iterators are two important concepts in Python that allow you to work with large amounts of data efficiently. In this article, we'll explore how generators and iterators work, and how you can use them to write more efficient and readable code.

Introduction to Generators and Iterators

Iterators are objects that allow you to traverse a sequence of data, one element at a time. In Python, iterators are implemented as classes that define two methods: __iter__() and __next__(). The __iter__() method returns the iterator object itself, and the __next__() method returns the next element in the sequence.

Generators are a type of iterator that are defined using a special syntax. Instead of defining a class that implements the __iter__() and __next__() methods, you define a function that uses the yield keyword to return a sequence of values one at a time.

Here's an example of a generator function that generates a sequence of Fibonacci numbers:

```python
def fibonacci():
    a, b = 0, 1
    while True:
        yield a
        a, b = b, a + b
```

In this example, the fibonacci() function is a generator that yields a sequence of Fibonacci numbers. Each time the yield keyword is encountered, the function returns the current value of a and then suspends execution until the next value is requested.

Using Generators and Iterators in Python

Generators and iterators are used extensively in Python to work with large datasets efficiently. They allow you to process data one element at a time, which can save memory and improve performance.

Here's an example of how to use a generator to process a large CSV file:

```python
import csv

def read_csv(filename):
    with open(filename, 'r') as f:
        reader = csv.reader(f)
        next(reader) # skip header
```

```
for row in reader:
    yield row
```

In this example, the read_csv() function is a generator that reads a CSV file one row at a time. The csv.reader() function returns an iterator that yields each row as a list of strings. The next() function is used to skip the header row, and the yield keyword is used to return each row as it is read from the file.

Benefits of Generators and Iterators

Generators and iterators offer several benefits in Python. First, they allow you to work with large datasets efficiently by processing data one element at a time. This can save memory and improve performance, especially when working with datasets that are too large to fit in memory.

Second, they allow you to write more readable and maintainable code by separating the logic for processing data from the logic for iterating over it. This can make your code easier to understand and modify, especially when working with complex data structures.

Finally, they allow you to create reusable code by encapsulating the logic for processing data in a generator or iterator. This can make your code more modular and easier to reuse in other projects.

Generators and iterators are two important concepts in Python that allow you to work with large amounts of data efficiently. They offer several benefits over traditional data processing techniques, including improved performance, readability, and modularity. By learning how to use generators and iterators, you can greatly enhance your programming skills and create more efficient and reusable code.

List comprehensions

List comprehensions are a concise and efficient way to create lists in Python. They allow you to create a new list by applying an expression to each element of an existing list, while also providing the ability to filter elements based on a condition. In this article, we'll explore the basics of list comprehensions and show you how to use them in your Python code.

Understanding List Comprehensions

List comprehensions are a compact way to create a new list by applying a transformation to each element of an existing list. The basic syntax for a list comprehension is:

[expression for item in iterable]

In this syntax, expression is the transformation to apply to each element of iterable, and item is the name of the variable that represents each element of iterable. iterable is any object that can be iterated over, such as a list, tuple, or string.

Here's an example of a simple list comprehension that squares each element of a list:

```
numbers = [1, 2, 3, 4, 5]
squares = [x ** 2 for x in numbers]
print(squares) # [1, 4, 9, 16, 25]
```

In this example, the list comprehension [x ** 2 for x in numbers] applies the transformation x ** 2 to each element x of the list numbers, resulting in a new list of squared numbers.

Filtering with List Comprehensions

In addition to transforming each element of an existing list, list comprehensions also provide the ability to filter elements based on a condition. The syntax for a filtered list comprehension is:

[expression for item in iterable if condition]

In this syntax, condition is a boolean expression that is evaluated for each element of iterable. Only elements for which condition evaluates to True are included in the new list.

Here's an example of a filtered list comprehension that only includes even numbers from a list:

```
numbers = [1, 2, 3, 4, 5]
evens = [x for x in numbers if x % 2 == 0]
print(evens) # [2, 4]
```

In this example, the filtered list comprehension [x for x in numbers if x % 2 == 0] includes only those elements x of the list numbers for which x % 2 == 0 is True, resulting in a new list of even numbers.

Nested List Comprehensions

List comprehensions can also be nested, allowing you to create more complex transformations and filters. The syntax for a nested list comprehension is:

[expression for item in iterable1 if condition1 for item2 in iterable2 if condition2]

In this syntax, condition1 is a boolean expression that is evaluated for each element of iterable1. Only elements for which condition1 evaluates to True are included in the new list. item2 and iterable2 are a nested item and iterable, respectively, that are evaluated for each element that passes condition1. condition2 is a boolean expression that is evaluated for each element of iterable2.

Here's an example of a nested list comprehension that generates all pairs of numbers from two lists:

```
numbers = [1, 2, 3]
letters = ['a', 'b', 'c']
pairs = [(x, y) for x in numbers for y in letters]
print(pairs) # [(1, 'a'), (1, 'b'), (1, 'c'), (2, 'a'), (2, 'b'), (2, 'c'), (3, 'a'), (3, 'b'), (3, 'c')]
```

In this example, the nested list comprehension [(x, y) for x in numbers for y in letters] generates all pairs of numbers and letters, resulting in a list of tuples.

List comprehensions are a powerful and concise way to create lists in Python. They allow you to apply a transformation to each element of an existing list, as well as filter elements based on a condition. They can also be nested to create more complex transformations and filters. By using list comprehensions in your code, you can write more efficient and expressive Python programs.

Sets and dictionaries

Sets and dictionaries are two important data structures in Python that can be used to store and manipulate collections of data. While both sets and dictionaries are similar in some ways, they have different properties and use cases. In this article, we'll explore the basics of sets and dictionaries in Python, and show you how to use them in your code.

Understanding Sets

A set is an unordered collection of unique elements. In Python, sets are created using curly braces {} or the set() function. Here's an example of creating a set of integers:

```
numbers = {1, 2, 3, 4, 5}
```

In this example, numbers is a set containing the integers 1, 2, 3, 4, and 5.

Adding and Removing Elements from Sets

Sets provide methods for adding and removing elements. The add() method adds a single element to a set, while the update() method can be used to add multiple elements. Here's an example of using these methods:

```
numbers = {1, 2, 3}
numbers.add(4)
print(numbers) # {1, 2, 3, 4}
numbers.update([5, 6])
print(numbers) # {1, 2, 3, 4, 5, 6}
```

In this example, we first add the integer 4 to the numbers set using the add() method. We then add the integers 5 and 6 to the numbers set using the update() method.

To remove an element from a set, you can use the remove() or discard() methods. The difference between these methods is that remove() will raise a KeyError if the element is not found in the set, while discard() will simply do nothing. Here's an example:

```
numbers = {1, 2, 3, 4, 5}
numbers.remove(4)
print(numbers) # {1, 2, 3, 5}
numbers.discard(6)
print(numbers) # {1, 2, 3, 5}
```

In this example, we first remove the integer 4 from the numbers set using the remove() method. We then attempt to remove the integer 6, which is not in the set, using the discard() method. Since 6 is not in the set, nothing happens.

Understanding Dictionaries

A dictionary is an unordered collection of key-value pairs, where each key is unique. In Python, dictionaries are created using curly braces {} or the dict() function. Here's an example of creating a dictionary of name and age:

```
person = {'Alice': 25, 'Bob': 30, 'Charlie': 35}
```

In this example, person is a dictionary containing three key-value pairs, where the keys are the names 'Alice', 'Bob', and 'Charlie', and the values are their ages.

Accessing and Modifying Dictionary Elements

You can access and modify elements in a dictionary using the keys. To access the value associated with a key, you can use the square bracket [] notation. Here's an example:

```
person = {'Alice': 25, 'Bob': 30, 'Charlie': 35}
print(person['Bob']) # 30
```

In this example, we access the value associated with the key 'Bob' in the person dictionary.

To modify the value associated with a key, you can simply assign a new value using the square bracket [] notation.

 Here's an example:

```
person = {'Alice': 25, 'Bob': 30}
person.update({'Charlie': 35, 'David': 40})
print(person) # {'Alice': 25, 'Bob': 30, 'Charlie': 35, 'David': 40}
```

In this example, we add two new key-value pairs, 'Charlie': 35 and 'David': 40, to the person dictionary using the update() method.

To remove a key-value pair from a dictionary, you can use the del keyword or the pop() method. The del keyword removes the key-value pair associated with a given key, while the pop() method removes the key-value pair associated with a given key and returns its value. Here's an example:

```
person = {'Alice': 25, 'Bob': 30, 'Charlie': 35}
del person['Bob']
print(person) # {'Alice': 25, 'Charlie': 35}
```

```
age = person.pop('Alice')
print(age) # 25
print(person) # {'Charlie': 35}
```

In this example, we first remove the key-value pair associated with the key 'Bob' from the person dictionary using the del keyword. We then remove the key-value pair associated with the key 'Alice' from the person dictionary using the pop() method and assign its value to the variable age.

Sets and dictionaries are two important data structures in Python that can be used to store and manipulate collections of data. Sets are useful for storing unique elements and performing set operations such as union, intersection, and difference. Dictionaries are useful for storing key-value pairs and performing lookups based on keys. By understanding the basics of sets and dictionaries, you can write more efficient and expressive Python code.

Tuples and sequences

In Python, tuples and sequences are two important data structures that are used to store collections of elements. Tuples are similar to lists, but they are immutable, which means that their contents cannot be modified once they are created. Sequences are a more general concept that includes both tuples and lists. In this article, we will explore the basics of tuples and sequences in Python, including how to create them, access their elements, and perform operations on them.

Creating Tuples and Sequences

Tuples are created by enclosing a sequence of elements in parentheses, separated by commas. Here's an example:

```
t = (1, 2, 3)
print(t) # (1, 2, 3)
```

In this example, we create a tuple t containing the elements 1, 2, and 3.

Sequences can also be created using the tuple() function or by converting a list to a tuple using the tuple() function. Here are some examples:

```
t = tuple([1, 2, 3])
print(t) # (1, 2, 3)

t = tuple("hello")
print(t) # ('h', 'e', 'l', 'l', 'o')
```

In the first example, we create a tuple t containing the elements 1, 2, and 3 by converting a list to a tuple using the tuple() function. In the second example, we create a tuple t containing the characters of the string "hello".

Accessing Elements of Tuples and Sequences

Elements of tuples and sequences can be accessed using indexing and slicing. Indexing is used to access a single element of a tuple or sequence, while slicing is used to access a subsequence of elements. The syntax for indexing and slicing is the same as for lists. Here are some examples:

```
t = (1, 2, 3, 4, 5)
print(t[0]) # 1
print(t[-1]) # 5
```

```
print(t[1:3]) # (2, 3)
```

In this example, we create a tuple t containing the elements 1, 2, 3, 4, and 5. We then access the first element of t using the index 0, the last element of t using the index -1, and a subsequence of elements from the second element to the third element using slicing.

Performing Operations on Tuples and Sequences

Tuples and sequences can be used in the same way as lists to perform operations such as concatenation, repetition, and membership testing. However, because tuples are immutable, some operations such as sorting and appending are not available. Here are some examples:

```
t1 = (1, 2, 3)
t2 = (4, 5, 6)
t3 = t1 + t2
print(t3) # (1, 2, 3, 4, 5, 6)

t4 = t1 * 3
print(t4) # (1, 2, 3, 1, 2, 3, 1, 2, 3)

t5 = (1, 2, 3)
print(2 in t5) # True
print(4 in t5) # False
```

In this example, we create two tuples t1 and t2 containing the elements 1, 2, and 3 and 4, 5, and 6, respectively. We then concatenate t1 and `t2 using the + operator to create a new tuple t3 containing the elements 1, 2, 3, 4, 5, and 6. We also repeat t1 three times using the * operator to create a new tuple t4 containing the elements 1, 2, 3, 1, 2, 3, 1, and 2, 3. Finally, we test for membership in t5 using the in operator, which returns True if the element is in the tuple and False otherwise.

Tuples and sequences are useful data structures in Python for storing collections of elements. Tuples are immutable, which makes them useful for storing fixed data such as coordinates, while sequences are more general and can be used for storing any type of data. In this article, we covered the basics of creating tuples and sequences, accessing their elements, and performing operations on them.

- ## Data structures in Python

Data structures in Python are a fundamental concept for storing, organizing, and manipulating data. Python provides a wide range of built-in data structures, including lists, tuples, sets, dictionaries, and more. In this article, we will explore each of these data structures, their properties, and how they can be used in Python.

Lists

Lists are one of the most commonly used data structures in Python. A list is a collection of elements that can be of any type, including other lists. Lists are mutable, meaning that their elements can be added, removed, or modified. Here is an example of creating a list, accessing its elements, and modifying it:

```
# Creating a list
my_list = [1, 2, 3, 4, 5]

# Accessing elements of a list
print(my_list[0]) # 1
print(my_list[-1]) # 5

# Modifying elements of a list
my_list[0] = 0
my_list.append(6)
print(my_list) # [0, 2, 3, 4, 5, 6]
```

Tuples

Tuples are similar to lists but are immutable, meaning that their elements cannot be modified once they are created. Tuples are often used to store fixed data such as coordinates, dates, or phone numbers. Here is an example of creating a tuple, accessing its elements, and using tuple unpacking:

```
# Creating a tuple
my_tuple = (1, 2, 3)

# Accessing elements of a tuple
print(my_tuple[0]) # 1
print(my_tuple[-1]) # 3

# Tuple unpacking
```

```
x, y, z = my_tuple
print(x) # 1
print(y) # 2
print(z) # 3
```

Sets

Sets are unordered collections of unique elements. Sets can be used to perform set operations such as union, intersection, and difference. Here is an example of creating a set, adding and removing elements, and performing set operations:

```
# Creating a set
my_set = {1, 2, 3}

# Adding and removing elements of a set
my_set.add(4)
my_set.remove(1)
print(my_set) # {2, 3, 4}

# Set operations
my_set2 = {3, 4, 5}
print(my_set.union(my_set2)) # {2, 3, 4, 5}
print(my_set.intersection(my_set2)) # {3, 4}
print(my_set.difference(my_set2)) # {2}
```

Dictionaries

Dictionaries are collections of key-value pairs. Each key is associated with a value, which can be of any type. Dictionaries are often used to store data in a way that can be easily accessed using a unique identifier such as a name or an ID. Here is an example of creating a dictionary, accessing its values, and modifying it:

```
# Creating a dictionary
my_dict = {"name": "John", "age": 30}

# Accessing values of a dictionary
print(my_dict["name"]) # John
print(my_dict.get("age")) # 30

# Modifying values of a dictionary
my_dict["age"] = 31
my_dict["city"] = "New York"
print(my_dict) # {'name': 'John', 'age': 31, 'city': 'New York'}
```

Stack and Queue implementation in Python

Stacks and queues are two important abstract data types commonly used in computer science. They are used to store and manipulate data in various ways. In this article, we will explore the implementation of stacks and queues in Python.

Stacks

A stack is a collection of elements that supports two main operations: push and pop. Push adds an element to the top of the stack, and pop removes the top element from the stack. The last element added to the stack is the first element to be removed (LIFO: Last In, First Out). Stacks are used in various applications such as expression evaluation, backtracking, and parsing.

In Python, we can implement a stack using a list. Here is an example of a stack implementation in Python:

```python
class Stack:
    def __init__(self):
        self.stack = []

    def push(self, item):
        self.stack.append(item)

    def pop(self):
        return self.stack.pop()

    def is_empty(self):
        return len(self.stack) == 0

    def peek(self):
        return self.stack[-1]
```

In the above code, we have defined a class called Stack that has four methods: push, pop, is_empty, and peek. The push method adds an element to the top of the stack, the pop method removes the top element from the stack, the is_empty method checks whether the stack is empty, and the peek method returns the top element of the stack without removing it.

Queues

A queue is a collection of elements that supports two main operations: enqueue and dequeue. Enqueue adds an element to the rear of the queue, and dequeue removes an element from the front of the queue. The first element added to the queue is the first element to be removed

(FIFO: First In, First Out). Queues are used in various applications such as scheduling, resource allocation, and event handling.

In Python, we can implement a queue using a list. However, this is not very efficient because adding or removing elements from the front of the list requires shifting all the other elements. Therefore, it is better to use a deque (double-ended queue) from the collections module. Here is an example of a queue implementation using a deque:

```python
from collections import deque

class Queue:
    def __init__(self):
        self.queue = deque()

    def enqueue(self, item):
        self.queue.append(item)

    def dequeue(self):
        return self.queue.popleft()

    def is_empty(self):
        return len(self.queue) == 0

    def peek(self):
        return self.queue[0]
```

In the above code, we have defined a class called Queue that has four methods: enqueue, dequeue, is_empty, and peek. The enqueue method adds an element to the rear of the queue, the dequeue method removes an element from the front of the queue, the is_empty method checks whether the queue is empty, and the peek method returns the front element of the queue without removing it.

In this article, we have explored the implementation of stacks and queues in Python. Stacks are useful for storing and manipulating data in a Last In, First Out (LIFO) manner, while queues are useful for storing and manipulating data in a First In, First Out (FIFO) manner. By using the code examples provided, you can easily implement these data structures in your own Python projects.

Binary trees and graphs in Python

Binary trees and graphs are important data structures used in computer science and are used to represent and manipulate various types of data. In this article, we will explore the implementation of binary trees and graphs in Python.

Binary Trees

A binary tree is a tree data structure where each node has at most two child nodes, referred to as the left and right child nodes. The first node of the tree is known as the root node. Binary trees are used in various applications such as searching and sorting algorithms, expression evaluation, and decision making.

In Python, we can implement a binary tree using classes. Here is an example of a binary tree implementation in Python:

```python
class Node:
    def __init__(self, value):
        self.value = value
        self.left_child = None
        self.right_child = None

class BinaryTree:
    def __init__(self, root):
        self.root = Node(root)

    def print_tree(self, traversal_type):
        if traversal_type == "inorder":
            return self.inorder_traversal(self.root, "")
        elif traversal_type == "preorder":
            return self.preorder_traversal(self.root, "")
        elif traversal_type == "postorder":
            return self.postorder_traversal(self.root, "")
        else:
            print("Traversal type " + str(traversal_type) + " is not supported.")

    def inorder_traversal(self, start, traversal):
        if start:
            traversal = self.inorder_traversal(start.left_child, traversal)
            traversal += (str(start.value) + "-")
            traversal = self.inorder_traversal(start.right_child, traversal)
        return traversal

    def preorder_traversal(self, start, traversal):
        if start:
```

```
        traversal += (str(start.value) + "-")
        traversal = self.preorder_traversal(start.left_child, traversal)
        traversal = self.preorder_traversal(start.right_child, traversal)
    return traversal

def postorder_traversal(self, start, traversal):
    if start:
        traversal = self.postorder_traversal(start.left_child, traversal)
        traversal = self.postorder_traversal(start.right_child, traversal)
        traversal += (str(start.value) + "-")
    return traversal
```

In the above code, we have defined two classes, Node and BinaryTree. The Node class represents a single node in the binary tree and has three attributes: value, left_child, and right_child. The BinaryTree class represents the binary tree and has four methods: print_tree, inorder_traversal, preorder_traversal, and postorder_traversal. The print_tree method is used to print the tree in a specific order, the inorder_traversal method traverses the tree in order, the preorder_traversal method traverses the tree in pre-order, and the postorder_traversal method traverses the tree in post-order.

Graphs

A graph is a collection of vertices (nodes) and edges that connect these vertices. Graphs are used in various applications such as social networks, transportation networks, and computer networks.

In Python, we can implement a graph using a dictionary. Here is an example of a graph implementation in Python:

```
class Graph:
    def __init__(self):
        self.graph_dict = {}

    def add_vertex(self, vertex):
        if vertex not in self.graph_dict:
            self.graph_dict[vertex] = []

    def add_edge(self, vertex1, vertex2):
        if vertex1 in self.graph_dict:
            self.graph_dict[vertex1].append(vertex2)
        else:
            self.graph_dict[vertex1] = [vertex2]

    def display_graph(self):
        print(self.graph_dict
```

In the above code, we have defined a class Graph that has three methods: add_vertex, add_edge, and display_graph. The add_vertex method is used to add a vertex to the graph, the add_edge method is used to add an edge between two vertices, and the display_graph method is used to display the graph.

Here is an example of how to use the Graph class to create and display a graph:

```
g = Graph()
g.add_vertex('A')
g.add_vertex('B')
g.add_vertex('C')
g.add_vertex('D')
g.add_vertex('E')

g.add_edge('A', 'B')
g.add_edge('B', 'C')
g.add_edge('C', 'D')
g.add_edge('D', 'E')
g.add_edge('E', 'A')

g.display_graph()
```

Output:

{'A': ['B', 'E'], 'B': ['C'], 'C': ['D'], 'D': ['E'], 'E': ['A']}

In the above example, we first create an instance of the Graph class and then add five vertices to it using the add_vertex method. We then add five edges between these vertices using the add_edge method. Finally, we display the graph using the display_graph method.

In this article, we explored the implementation of binary trees and graphs in Python. Binary trees are used to represent and manipulate various types of data, and graphs are used to represent the relationships between different objects. With the help of the code examples provided, you can easily implement binary trees and graphs in your Python programs.

Recursion in Python

Recursion in Python: A Comprehensive Guide to Writing Recursive Functions

Recursion is a powerful concept in computer programming that allows a function to call itself. In Python, recursion is often used to solve problems that can be broken down into smaller, simpler problems. In this article, we will explore the basics of recursion, how it works in Python, and provide examples of recursive functions.

What is Recursion?

Recursion is a technique where a function calls itself to solve a problem. When a function calls itself, it creates a new instance of that function with its own set of variables. The new instance of the function then runs, and can call itself again if necessary. This process continues until the function reaches a base case, where it no longer needs to call itself.

A recursive function consists of two parts: the base case and the recursive case. The base case is the terminating condition that stops the recursion. The recursive case is the condition that calls the function again with a simpler version of the problem.

Recursive Functions in Python

In Python, a recursive function is defined like any other function, with the addition of a recursive call to itself. For example, let's say we want to write a function that calculates the factorial of a number using recursion. The factorial of a number is the product of all positive integers up to and including that number.

We can define the factorial function recursively as follows:

```python
def factorial(n):
    if n == 1:
        return 1
    else:
        return n * factorial(n-1)
```

In this function, the base case is when n is equal to 1. When n equals 1, the function returns 1, which stops the recursion. If n is not equal to 1, the function calls itself with n-1 as the argument. The result of this call is multiplied by n and returned.

To see how this function works, let's call it with the argument 5:

```python
factorial(5)
```

The function first checks if 5 is equal to 1. Since it is not, the function calls itself with the argument 4. The new instance of the function checks if 4 is equal to 1, and since it is not, it calls itself with the argument 3. This process continues until the function reaches the base case, where n equals 1. The function then returns the result of the last multiplication, which is 5 * 4 * 3 * 2 * 1, or 120.

Another example of a recursive function is the Fibonacci sequence. The Fibonacci sequence is a series of numbers in which each number is the sum of the two preceding numbers. The first two numbers in the sequence are 0 and 1.

We can define the Fibonacci sequence recursively as follows:

```
def fibonacci(n):
    if n == 0:
        return 0
    elif n == 1:
        return 1
    else:
        return fibonacci(n-1) + fibonacci(n-2)
```

In this function, the base cases are when n is equal to 0 or 1. If n is equal to 0, the function returns 0. If n is equal to 1, the function returns 1. If n is not equal to 0 or 1, the function calls itself twice with n-1 and n-2 as the arguments. The results of these calls are added together and returned.

To see how this function works, let's call it with the argument 6:

fibonacci(6)

The function first checks if 6 is equal to 0 or 1. Since it is not, the function calls itself twice with the arguments 5 and 4. The new instances of the function call themselves with smaller values until they reach the base cases of 0 or 1. The results of these calls are added together and returned up the chain until the original call to fibonacci(6) returns the value 8.

Common Pitfalls with Recursion

Recursion can be a powerful tool in Python, but it can also lead to some common pitfalls. One of the most common pitfalls is the risk of infinite recursion. This occurs when a function never reaches its base case and continues to call itself indefinitely. This can cause the program to crash or run out of memory.

To avoid infinite recursion, it is important to ensure that each recursive call moves the function closer to the base case. In addition, it is important to choose appropriate base cases to ensure that the function will eventually terminate.

Another pitfall is the risk of stack overflow. Since each recursive call creates a new instance of the function, the function call stack can quickly become very deep. This can cause the program to run out of stack memory and crash.

To avoid stack overflow, it is important to use tail recursion. Tail recursion occurs when the final instruction of a function is a recursive call. In this case, the compiler or interpreter can optimize the code to avoid creating new stack frames, which reduces the risk of stack overflow.

Recursion is a powerful tool in Python that allows functions to call themselves to solve problems. Recursive functions consist of a base case and a recursive case, and are often used to solve problems that can be broken down into smaller, simpler problems.

However, recursion can also lead to common pitfalls such as infinite recursion and stack overflow. To avoid these pitfalls, it is important to ensure that each recursive call moves the function closer to the base case, and to use tail recursion when possible.

By understanding the basics of recursion and how to avoid common pitfalls, you can use this powerful technique to solve complex problems in your Python programs.

Debugging in Python

Debugging in Python: Tips and Techniques for Finding and Fixing Bugs

Debugging is an essential part of software development. Even the most experienced programmers make mistakes, and it is important to be able to find and fix bugs in your code. In this article, we will explore some tips and techniques for debugging in Python.

Understanding Errors in Python

Before we dive into the tips and techniques for debugging, it is important to understand the types of errors that can occur in Python.

Syntax errors occur when the Python interpreter cannot parse your code. These errors are often caused by typos, missing parentheses, or other syntax errors. Python will raise a SyntaxError and provide a message indicating where the error occurred.

```
# Example of a syntax error
print "Hello World!"
```

Name errors occur when you try to use a variable or function that has not been defined. Python will raise a NameError and provide a message indicating which name is not defined.

```
# Example of a name error
print(x)
```

Type errors occur when you try to use an object of the wrong type. Python will raise a TypeError and provide a message indicating which types are involved.

```
# Example of a type error
print("The answer is " + 42)
```

Debugging Techniques in Python

Now that we understand the types of errors that can occur in Python, let's explore some tips and techniques for debugging.

Use print statements

One of the simplest and most effective debugging techniques is to use print statements to output the value of variables at various points in your code. This can help you understand how your code is executing and identify where the problem is occurring.

```
# Example of using print statements
x = 10
y = 20
print("x = ", x)
print("y = ", y)
result = x + y
print("result = ", result)
```

Use a debugger

Python provides a built-in debugger called pdb that can be used to step through your code and identify where the problem is occurring. The debugger allows you to set breakpoints, view the value of variables, and execute code line by line.

To use the debugger, you can import the pdb module and call the set_trace() function at the point where you want to start debugging.

```
# Example of using the pdb debugger
import pdb

def multiply(x, y):
    result = x * y
    pdb.set_trace()
    return result

multiply(2, 3)
```

When the set_trace() function is called, the debugger will pause execution of the code and provide a prompt where you can enter commands to inspect variables and step through the code.

Use assertions

Assertions are statements that check whether a condition is true and raise an AssertionError if the condition is false. Assertions can be used to check that the input to a function is valid or that a particular condition holds true at a certain point in your code.

```
# Example of using assertions
def divide(x, y):
    assert y != 0, "Cannot divide by zero"
    return x / y

result = divide(10, 2)
print(result)
result = divide(10, 0)
```

In this example, the assert statement checks whether y is not equal to 0 and raises an AssertionError if it is. This can help you identify errors in your code and provide helpful error messages for users.

Debugging is an essential part of software development, and Python provides a variety of tools and techniques for finding and fixing bugs in your code. By using print statements, debuggers, and assertions, you can identify and resolve errors in your code and improve the quality of your software.

Testing in Python

Testing in Python: Techniques for Ensuring Code Quality

As a software developer, it is important to ensure that your code is high-quality and free of bugs. One of the best ways to do this is through testing. In this article, we will explore the basics of testing in Python, including techniques for writing and executing tests.

Why Test Your Code?

Testing is a critical part of the software development process. It helps ensure that your code is functioning correctly and that it will continue to function as expected even as you make changes to it. Without testing, bugs and errors can go undetected, leading to more serious problems down the line.

Types of Tests in Python

There are several types of tests that can be performed in Python:

Unit Tests: These tests focus on individual units or functions in your code. They are designed to test the behavior of a single piece of code in isolation.

Integration Tests: These tests focus on the interaction between different components or modules in your code. They are designed to test how these components work together.

Functional Tests: These tests focus on the behavior of your code from the perspective of the user. They are designed to test the entire system, from input to output.

Writing Tests in Python

To write tests in Python, you will typically use a testing framework such as pytest or unittest. These frameworks provide a set of tools and functions for writing and executing tests.

Here is an example of a simple test using pytest:

```
# Example of a test using pytest
def test_addition():
    assert 2 + 2 == 4
```

In this example, we define a test called test_addition that checks whether 2 + 2 equals 4. We use the assert statement to check this condition and pytest will report whether the test passed or failed.

Executing Tests in Python

Once you have written your tests, you can execute them using the testing framework. To do this, you typically run a command such as pytest or python -m unittest.

Here is an example of running tests using pytest:

In this example, we run the pytest command and specify the name of the file containing our tests.

Best Practices for Testing in Python

To ensure that your tests are effective and useful, there are several best practices to keep in mind:

Write tests for all of your code: Make sure that you write tests for every function or module in your code.

Use descriptive test names: Use descriptive names for your tests so that it is clear what they are testing.

Test edge cases: Make sure that your tests cover edge cases and unusual input values.

Run tests frequently: Make sure that you run your tests frequently, especially after making changes to your code.

Testing is an essential part of the software development process, and Python provides a variety of tools and frameworks for writing and executing tests. By following best practices and writing comprehensive tests, you can ensure that your code is high-quality and free of bugs.

Debugging and profiling Python applications

Debugging and Profiling Python Applications: Tips and Techniques

Debugging and profiling are essential tools for any software developer. In this article, we will explore some tips and techniques for debugging and profiling Python applications.

Debugging Python Applications

Debugging is the process of identifying and fixing errors in your code. Python provides several tools and techniques for debugging your applications.

Using print statements: One of the simplest ways to debug your code is by using print statements. By adding print statements to your code, you can see the values of variables and the flow of your program.

```
# Example of using print statements for debugging
def add(a, b):
    print("Adding", a, "and", b)
    result = a + b
    print("Result:", result)
    return result
```

Using pdb: The Python Debugger (pdb) is a powerful tool for debugging your code. It allows you to step through your code line by line and examine the values of variables.

```
# Example of using pdb for debugging
import pdb

def add(a, b):
    pdb.set_trace()
    result = a + b
    return result
```

Using logging: The logging module in Python allows you to log messages at different levels of severity. By using logging, you can easily trace the flow of your program and identify errors.

```
# Example of using logging for debugging
import logging

def add(a, b):
    logging.debug("Adding %s and %s", a, b)
    result = a + b
    logging.debug("Result: %s", result)
    return result
```

Profiling Python Applications

Profiling is the process of analyzing the performance of your code. It allows you to identify the parts of your code that are slow and optimize them.

Using cProfile: The cProfile module in Python provides a way to profile your code at the function level. It allows you to see how much time is spent in each function and how many times each function is called.

```python
# Example of using cProfile for profiling
import cProfile

def main():
    # Code to be profiled goes here
    pass

if __name__ == '__main__':
    cProfile.run('main()')
```

Using line_profiler: The line_profiler module in Python provides a way to profile your code at the line level. It allows you to see how much time is spent on each line of code.

```python
# Example of using line_profiler for profiling
!pip install line_profiler

%load_ext line_profiler

@profile
def add(a, b):
    result = a + b
    return result
```

Using memory_profiler: The memory_profiler module in Python provides a way to profile the memory usage of your code. It allows you to see how much memory is used by each line of code.

```python
# Example of using memory_profiler for profiling
!pip install memory_profiler

%load_ext memory_profiler

@profile
def add(a, b):
    result = a + b
    return result
```

Debugging and profiling are essential tools for any software developer. Python provides several tools and techniques for debugging and profiling your applications. By using these tools and techniques, you can identify and fix errors in your code and optimize its performance.

Virtual Environments in Python: A Comprehensive Guide

Python is a popular programming language used in various fields such as web development, data science, and machine learning. When developing applications using Python, it is essential to maintain the dependencies and versions of the packages used. Virtual environments provide a solution to this problem by creating an isolated environment for each project. This guide will cover everything you need to know about virtual environments in Python.

What are Virtual Environments?

Virtual environments are isolated environments created specifically for a project. They allow developers to install specific versions of Python and packages without affecting the system-level Python installation. This isolation prevents conflicts between packages and enables the creation of reproducible development environments.

Creating Virtual Environments

Python comes with a built-in module for creating virtual environments called venv. Here's how you can create a virtual environment:

```
python -m venv myenv
```

The above command creates a virtual environment named myenv. Once created, you can activate the virtual environment using the following command:

```
source myenv/bin/activate
```

Managing Packages in Virtual Environments

Once you have activated the virtual environment, you can install packages just like you would in a system-level Python installation. However, the packages will be installed only in the virtual environment and not in the system-level installation. Here's an example of installing the NumPy package in a virtual environment:

```
pip install numpy
```

Freezing Requirements

It's a good practice to freeze the requirements of your project, including the version of Python and packages used, to ensure reproducibility. You can do this using the pip freeze command:

```
pip freeze > requirements.txt
```

This command creates a file named requirements.txt that contains a list of all the packages installed in the virtual environment along with their versions.

Sharing Virtual Environments

Virtual environments can be shared with other developers to ensure that they can reproduce your development environment. You can share your virtual environment by creating a requirements.txt file and sharing it along with the codebase.

Here's how another developer can create the same virtual environment as yours:

```
python -m venv myenv
source myenv/bin/activate
pip install -r requirements.txt
```

Managing Multiple Virtual Environments

When working on multiple projects, it's essential to maintain separate virtual environments for each project. You can create multiple virtual environments by specifying a different name for each environment:

```
python -m venv project1
python -m venv project2
```

To activate a specific virtual environment, use the source command with the path to the virtual environment's activation script:

```
source project1/bin/activate
```

Virtual environments provide an efficient and practical way to manage dependencies and versions of packages used in a Python project. They enable the creation of isolated development environments that are reproducible and free from package conflicts. With the venv module, creating and managing virtual environments is easy and straightforward. By using virtual environments, you can ensure that your Python applications are portable and can be easily shared with other developers.

Concurrency in Python: A Practical Guide

Concurrency is the ability of a program to execute multiple tasks simultaneously. Python provides several mechanisms for achieving concurrency, including threading, multiprocessing, and asynchronous programming. In this guide, we will explore each of these mechanisms and discuss when to use each one.

Threading

Threading is a mechanism for achieving concurrency by running multiple threads within a single process. Each thread can execute a different task simultaneously, allowing for improved performance and responsiveness. Here's an example of using threading in Python:

```python
import threading

def worker():
    """Thread worker function"""
    print('Worker thread started')
    # Do some work here
    print('Worker thread finished')

# Create a new thread
thread = threading.Thread(target=worker)
# Start the thread
thread.start()

# Wait for the thread to finish
thread.join()

print('Main thread finished')
```

The above code creates a new thread and starts it using the start() method. The join() method is called to wait for the thread to finish before continuing execution.

Multiprocessing

Multiprocessing is a mechanism for achieving concurrency by running multiple processes in parallel. Each process runs in its own memory space, providing isolation and security. Here's an example of using multiprocessing in Python:

```python
import multiprocessing

def worker():
    """Process worker function"""
    print('Worker process started')
    # Do some work here
    print('Worker process finished')

# Create a new process
process = multiprocessing.Process(target=worker)
# Start the process
process.start()

# Wait for the process to finish
process.join()

print('Main process finished')
```

The above code creates a new process and starts it using the start() method. The join() method is called to wait for the process to finish before continuing execution.

Asynchronous Programming

Asynchronous programming is a mechanism for achieving concurrency by allowing a program to perform multiple tasks simultaneously without creating additional threads or processes. This is achieved using coroutines and event loops. Here's an example of using asynchronous programming in Python:

```python
import asyncio

async def worker():
    """Coroutine worker function"""
    print('Worker coroutine started')
    # Do some work here
    print('Worker coroutine finished')

# Create a new event loop
loop = asyncio.get_event_loop()

# Schedule the coroutine to run
loop.run_until_complete(worker())

print('Main coroutine finished')
```

The above code creates a new event loop and schedules a coroutine to run using the run_until_complete() method. The event loop manages the execution of the coroutine and switches between tasks as needed.

Concurrency is an essential feature of modern programming languages and is essential for building high-performance applications. Python provides several mechanisms for achieving concurrency, including threading, multiprocessing, and asynchronous programming. Each mechanism has its own advantages and disadvantages, and the choice of mechanism will depend on the specific requirements of your application. By understanding the different mechanisms for achieving concurrency in Python, you can build more efficient and responsive applications.

Multiprocessing in Python: A Comprehensive Guide

Multiprocessing is a technique for parallel processing in which multiple processes are spawned to perform a task. In Python, the multiprocessing module provides a way to create and manage child processes that can run concurrently with the main process. This can be a powerful tool for speeding up computation-heavy tasks and achieving true parallelism.

In this guide, we will explore the multiprocessing module in Python and demonstrate how it can be used to improve performance in your Python applications.

Chapter 1: Getting Started with Multiprocessing

The multiprocessing module provides a way to create and manage child processes in Python. To get started, we first need to import the module:

```
import multiprocessing
```

Next, we can create a new process using the Process class:

```
def my_function():
    print('Hello from child process!')

process = multiprocessing.Process(target=my_function)
process.start()
```

In the above code, we define a function my_function() which will be run by the child process. We then create a new process using the Process class and pass our function as the target. Finally, we start the process using the start() method.

Chapter 2: Communication Between Processes

When using multiprocessing, it's often necessary to share data between the main process and child processes. The multiprocessing module provides several ways to achieve this, including pipes, queues, and shared memory.

Here's an example of using a Queue to share data between a parent and child process:

```
def my_function(queue):
    data = queue.get()
    print('Received:', data)

queue = multiprocessing.Queue()
queue.put('Hello from parent process!')
```

```
process = multiprocessing.Process(target=my_function, args=(queue,))
process.start()
```

In the above code, we create a Queue object and put some data into it. We then pass the queue as an argument to our child process function, my_function(). The child process retrieves the data from the queue using the get() method.

Chapter 3: Parallel Processing with Pool

The multiprocessing module provides a Pool class which can be used to create a pool of worker processes that can execute tasks in parallel. Here's an example of using Pool to execute a function on a list of inputs:

```
def my_function(input):
    return input ** 2

inputs = [1, 2, 3, 4, 5]
pool = multiprocessing.Pool()
results = pool.map(my_function, inputs)
```

In the above code, we define a function my_function() which takes an input and returns its square. We then create a list of inputs and a new Pool object. Finally, we use the map() method of the Pool object to execute our function on each input in parallel.

Chapter 4: Synchronization with Locks and Semaphores

When using multiprocessing, it's important to ensure that multiple processes don't access shared resources simultaneously. The multiprocessing module provides two synchronization primitives, locks and semaphores, which can be used to achieve this.

Here's an example of using a lock to synchronize access to a shared variable:

```
def my_function(lock, shared_variable):
    lock.acquire()
    shared_variable.value += 1
    lock.release()

lock = multiprocessing.Lock()
shared_variable = multiprocessing.Value('i', 0)

processes = []
for i in range(10):
    process = multiprocessing.Process(target=my_function, args=(lock, shared_variable))
    processes.append(process)
    process.start()
```

```
for process in processes:
    process.join()

print('Final value:', shared_variable.value)
```

In the above code, we define a function my_function() which increments a shared variable.

We create a new lock object using the Lock class and a shared variable using the Value class. We then create ten processes, each of which executes my_function() with the lock and shared variable as arguments. Finally, we wait for all processes to complete and print the final value of the shared variable.

Chapter 5: Process Pools with the multiprocessing module

The multiprocessing module also provides a Pool class that can be used to create a pool of worker processes that can be used to execute tasks in parallel.

```
from multiprocessing import Pool

def my_function(x):
    return x**2

if __name__ == '__main__':
    with Pool(processes=4) as pool:
        results = pool.map(my_function, range(10))
    print(results)
```

In the above code, we create a new Pool object with four worker processes using the with statement. We then use the map() method to apply the my_function() function to the range of integers from 0 to 9, in parallel. Finally, we print the results.

Chapter 6: Using the concurrent.futures module

The concurrent.futures module is another option for creating parallel processes in Python. This module provides a high-level interface for asynchronously executing functions using threads or processes.

```
from concurrent.futures import ProcessPoolExecutor

def my_function(x):
    return x**2

if __name__ == '__main__':
    with ProcessPoolExecutor(max_workers=4) as executor:
        results = executor.map(my_function, range(10))
```

```
print(list(results))
```

In the above code, we use the ProcessPoolExecutor class to create a pool of four worker processes. We then use the map() method to apply the my_function() function to the range of integers from 0 to 9, in parallel. Finally, we print the results.

Chapter 7: Conclusion

In this guide, we have explored the multiprocessing module in Python and demonstrated how it can be used to improve performance in your Python applications. We have covered a range of topics, including communication between processes, parallel processing with Pool, and synchronization with locks and semaphores.

By leveraging multiprocessing, you can make your Python applications more efficient and take full advantage of modern hardware. Whether you're working with large datasets or building complex simulations, multiprocessing is a powerful tool that can help you get the job done faster.

Threading in Python

Chapter 1: Introduction to Threading in Python

Python provides several ways to implement concurrency and parallelism in your programs. One of the most popular ways is through threading. Threading allows you to execute multiple threads of execution within a single process.

In this guide, we will explore threading in Python and learn how to use it to make your applications more efficient.

Chapter 2: The threading module

The threading module is the primary module for threading in Python. It provides a simple and efficient way to create and manage threads.

```
import threading

def my_function():
    print('Hello from thread', threading.current_thread().name)

if __name__ == '__main__':
    thread = threading.Thread(target=my_function)
    thread.start()
    print('Hello from main thread')
    thread.join()
```

In the above code, we create a new thread using the Thread class and the target parameter. We then start the thread using the start() method and wait for it to complete using the join() method. Finally, we print a message from the main thread and the thread we created.

Chapter 3: Sharing Data between Threads

Threads can share data between each other by using shared variables. However, if multiple threads try to access and modify the same variable simultaneously, it can lead to race conditions and data corruption.

The threading module provides a few synchronization primitives, including locks and semaphores, that can be used to prevent race conditions and ensure data consistency.

```python
import threading

def increment(counter, lock):
    for _ in range(100000):
        with lock:
            counter.value += 1

if __name__ == '__main__':
    from multiprocessing import Value, Lock
    counter = Value('i', 0)
    lock = Lock()
    threads = [threading.Thread(target=increment, args=(counter, lock)) for _ in range(4)]
    for thread in threads:
        thread.start()
    for thread in threads:
        thread.join()
    print('Counter:', counter.value)
```

In the above code, we create a new Value object and a Lock object from the multiprocessing module. We then create four threads and pass the shared Value and Lock objects as arguments to the increment() function. We use the with statement to acquire and release the lock around the critical section of the code that modifies the shared variable.

Chapter 4: Threading with Queues

Queues can be used to coordinate work between threads. The queue module provides the Queue class, which is a thread-safe implementation of a queue.

```python
import queue
import threading

def worker(queue):
    while True:
        item = queue.get()
        if item is None:
            break
        print(item)

if __name__ == '__main__':
    q = queue.Queue()
    threads = [threading.Thread(target=worker, args=(q,)) for _ in range(4)]
    for thread in threads:
        thread.start()
    for i in range(10):
        q.put(i)
    for _ in range(4):
        q.put(None)
```

```
for thread in threads:
    thread.join()
```

In the above code, we create a new Queue object and four worker threads that consume items from the queue. We use the put() method to add items to the queue and the None object to signal the end of the work. We then use the join() method to wait for all threads to complete.

Asynchronous programming with asyncio

Chapter 1: Introduction to Asynchronous Programming with asyncio

Asynchronous programming is a way to write programs that can perform multiple tasks concurrently, without blocking the execution of the program. Python provides several ways to implement asynchronous programming, including asyncio.

In this guide, we will explore asyncio in Python and learn how to use it to make your applications more efficient.

Chapter 2: The asyncio module

The asyncio module is the primary module for asynchronous programming in Python. It provides a simple and efficient way to create and manage asynchronous tasks.

```python
import asyncio

async def my_coroutine():
    print('Hello from coroutine')

if __name__ == '__main__':
    loop = asyncio.get_event_loop()
    loop.run_until_complete(my_coroutine())
    loop.close()
```

In the above code, we create a new coroutine using the async keyword and the async def syntax. We then use the run_until_complete() method to execute the coroutine and the close() method to close the event loop.

Chapter 3: Asynchronous I/O

Asynchronous I/O is a way to perform I/O operations without blocking the execution of the program. The asyncio module provides several functions for performing I/O operations asynchronously, including asyncio.open_connection() and asyncio.start_server().

```python
import asyncio

async def handle_client(reader, writer):
    while True:
        data = await reader.read(1024)
        if not data:
```

```
            break
        writer.write(data)
        await writer.drain()
    writer.close()

if __name__ == '__main__':
    loop = asyncio.get_event_loop()
    server = loop.run_until_complete(asyncio.start_server(handle_client, 'localhost', 8888))
    try:
        loop.run_forever()
    except KeyboardInterrupt:
        pass
    server.close()
    loop.run_until_complete(server.wait_closed())
    loop.close()
```

In the above code, we create a server using the start_server() function and the handle_client() coroutine. We use the await keyword to perform asynchronous I/O operations on the client connection, including reading data and writing data back to the client.

Chapter 4: Asynchronous Tasks

Asynchronous tasks are a way to perform multiple tasks concurrently in an asynchronous program. The asyncio module provides several functions for creating and managing asynchronous tasks, including asyncio.create_task() and asyncio.gather().

```
import asyncio

async def my_task(name):
    print(f'Task {name} started')
    await asyncio.sleep(1)
    print(f'Task {name} finished')

if __name__ == '__main__':
    loop = asyncio.get_event_loop()
    tasks = [loop.create_task(my_task(i)) for i in range(5)]
    loop.run_until_complete(asyncio.gather(*tasks))
    loop.close()
```

In the above code, we create five asynchronous tasks using the create_task() function and the my_task() coroutine. We use the gather() function to wait for all tasks to complete before closing the event loop.

In this guide, we have explored asyncio in Python and learned how to use the asyncio module to create and manage asynchronous tasks and perform asynchronous I/O operations.

Asynchronous programming can make your applications more efficient and responsive, and asyncio provides a simple and efficient way to implement it in Python.

Networking in Python

Chapter 1: Introduction to Networking in Python

Python provides powerful networking capabilities that allow you to build a wide range of network applications. With Python, you can create applications that communicate over the internet, access remote resources, and share data between machines.

In this guide, we will explore networking in Python and learn how to use it to build robust and scalable network applications.

Chapter 2: Socket Programming in Python

Socket programming is a low-level networking interface that provides a way to communicate between computers over a network. Python provides a rich set of libraries for socket programming, including the socket module.

```python
import socket

HOST = 'localhost'
PORT = 5000

with socket.socket(socket.AF_INET, socket.SOCK_STREAM) as s:
    s.bind((HOST, PORT))
    s.listen()
    conn, addr = s.accept()
    with conn:
        print(f'Connected by {addr}')
        while True:
            data = conn.recv(1024)
            if not data:
                break
            conn.sendall(data)
```

In the above code, we create a socket object using the socket.socket() function and the AF_INET and SOCK_STREAM constants. We then bind the socket to a host and port, listen for incoming connections, and accept the connection. We use the recv() and sendall() methods to receive and send data over the socket.

Chapter 3: HTTP Programming in Python

HTTP is the protocol used for communicating between web clients and servers over the internet. Python provides several libraries for working with HTTP, including the http.client and urllib modules.

```
import http.client

conn = http.client.HTTPSConnection('www.python.org')
conn.request('GET', '/')
response = conn.getresponse()
print(response.status, response.reason)
data = response.read()
conn.close()
```

In the above code, we create an HTTPS connection to the Python website using the http.client.HTTPSConnection() function. We then send a GET request to retrieve the homepage and read the response data.

Chapter 4: Asynchronous Networking with asyncio

Asynchronous networking allows you to perform multiple network operations concurrently in a single thread, making your applications more efficient and responsive. Python provides several libraries for asynchronous networking, including the asyncio module.

```
import asyncio
import aiohttp

async def fetch(session, url):
    async with session.get(url) as response:
        return await response.text()

async def main():
    async with aiohttp.ClientSession() as session:
        html = await fetch(session, 'http://www.python.org')
        print(html)

if __name__ == '__main__':
    loop = asyncio.get_event_loop()
    loop.run_until_complete(main())
```

In the above code, we create an asynchronous HTTP client using the aiohttp library and the ClientSession object. We use the async with syntax to manage the session and the fetch() coroutine to perform an HTTP GET request and return the response text. We use the run_until_complete() method to run the main() coroutine.

Chapter 5: Conclusion

In this guide, we have explored networking in Python and learned how to use socket programming, HTTP programming, and asynchronous networking to build robust and scalable network applications. Python provides a rich set of libraries for networking, making it easy to create applications that communicate over the internet and share data between machines.

Working with APIs in Python

Introduction to APIs

Application Programming Interfaces (APIs) provide a way for software applications to communicate with each other. APIs allow developers to access and manipulate data from other software applications or services, making it easy to integrate different systems and build more powerful applications.

In this guide, we will explore how to work with APIs in Python and learn how to use them to build robust and scalable applications.

RESTful APIs

RESTful APIs are a popular type of API that use HTTP methods to perform operations on resources. REST APIs are stateless and use URIs to represent resources, making them easy to use and understand. Python provides several libraries for working with RESTful APIs, including the requests and http.client modules.

```python
import requests

response = requests.get('https://api.github.com/users/username/repos')
print(response.json())
```

In the above code, we use the requests library to send a GET request to the GitHub API and retrieve information about the repositories owned by a user. We use the json() method to convert the response data to a Python object.

Authentication and Authorization

Many APIs require authentication and authorization to access their resources. Python provides several libraries for working with authentication, including the requests and oauthlib modules.

```python
import requests
from requests_oauthlib import OAuth1

url = 'https://api.twitter.com/1.1/account/verify_credentials.json'
auth = OAuth1('API_KEY', 'API_SECRET', 'ACCESS_TOKEN', 'ACCESS_TOKEN_SECRET')
response = requests.get(url, auth=auth)
print(response.json())
```

In the above code, we use the requests_oauthlib library to authenticate with the Twitter API and retrieve information about the authenticated user. We use the OAuth1 class to provide the API key, secret, access token, and access token secret.

Using APIs with Data Science Libraries

Python provides powerful libraries for data science and machine learning, such as numpy, pandas, and scikit-learn. These libraries can be used with APIs to retrieve and analyze data.

```python
import requests
import pandas as pd

response = requests.get('https://api.coinmarketcap.com/v1/ticker/')
data = response.json()
df = pd.DataFrame(data)
print(df.head())
```

In the above code, we use the requests library to send a GET request to the CoinMarketCap API and retrieve information about cryptocurrency prices. We use the json() method to convert the response data to a Python object, and then create a pandas DataFrame to analyze the data.

In this guide, we have explored how to work with APIs in Python and learned how to use RESTful APIs, authentication and authorization, and data science libraries to build robust and scalable applications. APIs are a powerful tool for integrating different systems and building more powerful applications, and Python provides a rich set of libraries for working with APIs.

Web development in Python

Python is a versatile programming language that has been used for a wide range of applications, including web development. With its clean syntax, extensive libraries, and vast community, Python has become a popular choice for building web applications. In this news article, we will explore the latest developments in web development using Python.

Introduction to Web Development in Python

Web development involves creating websites, web applications, and web services that are accessed over the internet. Python provides several libraries and frameworks for web development, including Flask, Django, and Pyramid. These libraries and frameworks make it easy to build web applications quickly and efficiently.

Flask

Flask is a lightweight and flexible web framework for Python. Flask provides a simple and elegant way to create web applications and APIs. Flask comes with a built-in web server, making it easy to get started. Flask also supports a variety of extensions that can add functionality to your application, such as authentication, database integration, and more.

```
from flask import Flask

app = Flask(__name__)

@app.route('/')
def hello_world():
    return 'Hello, World!'

if __name__ == '__main__':
    app.run()
```

In the above code, we use Flask to create a simple web application that returns a "Hello, World!" message. We define a route using the @app.route() decorator, which maps the URL / to the hello_world() function.

Django

Django is a full-featured web framework for Python that is used by some of the largest websites in the world, including Instagram and Pinterest. Django provides a robust set of features for building complex web applications, including an ORM for working with databases, a templating engine for rendering HTML, and built-in security features.

```python
from django.http import HttpResponse
from django.shortcuts import render

    def hello_world(request):
        return HttpResponse("Hello, World!")

    def home(request):
        return render(request, 'home.html')
```

In the above code, we use Django to create two views: hello_world() and home(). The hello_world() view returns a simple message, while the home() view renders a template called home.html.

Pyramid

Pyramid is a flexible and scalable web framework for Python. Pyramid is designed to be modular, allowing developers to choose the components they need for their application. Pyramid supports a variety of databases and templating engines, making it a great choice for building complex web applications.

```python
from pyramid.config import Configurator
from pyramid.response import Response

def hello_world(request):
    return Response('Hello, World!')

if __name__ == '__main__':
    config = Configurator()
    config.add_route('hello', '/')
    config.add_view(hello_world, route_name='hello')
    app = config.make_wsgi_app()
    serve(app, host='0.0.0.0', port=8080)
```

In the above code, we use Pyramid to create a simple web application that returns a "Hello, World!" message. We define a route using the config.add_route() method and map it to the hello_world() function using the config.add_view() method. We then create a WSGI application using the config.make_wsgi_app() method and serve it using the serve() method.

Python provides a variety of libraries and frameworks for web development, each with its own strengths and weaknesses. Flask is a lightweight and flexible framework, Django is a full-featured framework for building complex web applications, and Pyramid is a scalable and modular framework. With Python, developers can build web applications quickly and efficiently, making it a great choice for web development.

Introduction to web frameworks (Flask, Django, Pyramid, etc.)

Web development is an essential aspect of modern-day technology. With the increasing demand for web-based applications, frameworks have emerged as a popular tool for web developers to create web applications with ease and speed. In this article, we will discuss the introduction to web frameworks, with a focus on Flask, Django, Pyramid, and other popular web frameworks.

What is a Web Framework?

A web framework is a software framework that helps developers create web applications by providing pre-built tools, templates, and libraries. Web frameworks help developers avoid repetitive tasks by providing reusable code blocks, so they can focus on implementing specific application requirements. The use of web frameworks reduces the development time, increases the productivity of developers, and ensures the maintainability of the codebase.

Types of Web Frameworks

There are two types of web frameworks:

Full-stack Frameworks: These frameworks provide all the components required to build a complete web application, including front-end, back-end, and database components. Django is an example of a full-stack framework.

Microframeworks: These frameworks provide only the bare minimum required to build a web application, and they leave the rest of the development up to the developer. Flask is an example of a microframework.

Introduction to Flask

Flask is a microframework for Python that is lightweight, easy to learn, and easy to use. Flask has a modular design and provides only the bare minimum required to build a web application. Flask is highly extensible and allows developers to use various extensions to add functionality to their application.

Flask uses the Jinja2 template engine to render HTML templates. Flask also provides support for database integration using various libraries like SQLAlchemy, Peewee, and Flask-SQLAlchemy. Flask supports different types of HTTP requests like GET, POST, PUT, DELETE, and more. Flask is suitable for building small to medium-sized web applications.

Introduction to Django

Django is a full-stack web framework for Python that is widely used in the industry. Django provides a robust framework for building web applications and follows the Model-View-Controller (MVC) architectural pattern. Django has a comprehensive set of tools that help developers create complex web applications quickly.

Django provides support for database integration using its Object-Relational Mapping (ORM) system. Django also has a built-in Admin interface that provides an easy way to manage data in the database. Django supports different types of HTTP requests and provides built-in support for authentication and authorization.

Introduction to Pyramid

Pyramid is a web framework for Python that is flexible, scalable, and highly extensible. Pyramid is based on the Model-View-Controller (MVC) architectural pattern and provides support for database integration using various libraries like SQLAlchemy, MongoEngine, and more.

Pyramid is highly configurable and provides a variety of configuration options for different use cases. Pyramid provides a minimalistic approach to building web applications and leaves most of the implementation details up to the developer. Pyramid is suitable for building small to large-sized web applications.

Web frameworks are essential tools for modern web development. Flask, Django, and Pyramid are some of the most popular web frameworks for Python, each with its own unique set of features and capabilities. When choosing a web framework, it is important to consider the requirements of the project and choose a framework that is suitable for the project's specific needs.

Using Flask for web development

Flask is a popular microframework for Python that is widely used for web development. Flask is lightweight, easy to use, and highly extensible, making it an ideal choice for building small to medium-sized web applications. In this article, we will provide an introduction to using Flask for web development, with a focus on its key features and how to use them.

Getting Started with Flask

To get started with Flask, you first need to install it. You can install Flask using pip, the package installer for Python, by running the following command in your terminal:

pip install flask

Once you have installed Flask, you can create a new Flask application by creating a new Python file and importing the Flask module. Here's an example of a simple Flask application:

from flask import Flask

```
app = Flask(__name__)

@app.route('/')
def hello():
    return 'Hello, World!'
```

In this example, we import the Flask module and create a new Flask application instance. We then define a route using the @app.route decorator, which specifies the URL path for the route. In this case, the route is /, which is the root path for the application. We then define a function that returns a string message when the route is accessed.

Running the Flask Application

To run the Flask application, you can use the flask run command in your terminal:

```
export FLASK_APP=hello.py
flask run
```

This will start a local web server on your machine that you can use to access your Flask application. You can access the application by navigating to http://localhost:5000 in your web browser.

Working with Templates

One of the key features of Flask is its support for templates, which are pre-built HTML files that can be used to generate dynamic content for web pages. Flask uses the Jinja2 templating engine, which is a powerful and flexible engine that provides a range of features for generating dynamic content.

Here's an example of using a template in Flask:

```python
from flask import Flask, render_template

app = Flask(__name__)

@app.route('/')
def hello():
    return render_template('index.html', name='John')

if __name__ == '__main__':
    app.run()
```

In this example, we import the render_template function from the Flask module and use it to render an HTML template file called index.html. We also pass a variable called name to the template, which is used to generate dynamic content. We then run the Flask application using the app.run() function.

Working with Forms

Flask also provides built-in support for handling web forms, which are used to collect user input from web pages. Flask uses the request object to access form data, which can be accessed using the request.form dictionary.

Here's an example of using a form in Flask:

```python
from flask import Flask, render_template, request

app = Flask(__name__)

@app.route('/', methods=['GET', 'POST'])
def form():
    if request.method == 'POST':
        name = request.form['name']
        return render_template('result.html', name=name)
    return render_template('form.html')

if __name__ == '__main__':
```

```
app.run()
```

In this example, we define a route that accepts both GET and POST requests. When the user submits the form, the POST method is used to send the form data to the server. We then access the form data using the request.form dictionary and use it to generate dynamic content in a template called result.html. If the request method is GET, we display a form for the user to fill out, which is defined in a separate template called form.html.

Working with Databases

Flask also provides support for working with databases, which are used to store and manage large amounts of structured data. Flask supports a range of different databases, including SQLite, MySQL, and PostgreSQL, among others.

Here's an example of using a database in Flask:

```
from flask import Flask, render_template, request
from flask_sqlalchemy import SQLAlchemy

app = Flask(__name__)
app.config['SQLALCHEMY_DATABASE_URI'] = 'sqlite:///test.db'
db = SQLAlchemy(app)

class User(db.Model):
    id = db.Column(db.Integer, primary_key=True)
    name = db.Column(db.String(80), nullable=False)

@app.route('/', methods=['GET', 'POST'])
def form():
    if request.method == 'POST':
        name = request.form['name']
        user = User(name=name)
        db.session.add(user)
        db.session.commit()
        return render_template('result.html', name=name)
    return render_template('form.html')

if __name__ == '__main__':
    db.create_all()
    app.run()
```

In this example, we first import the SQLAlchemy module and use it to create a new database instance. We then define a User model that defines the structure of the data to be stored in the database. We also define a route that uses the User model to add new data to the database when the user submits the form.

Using Django for web development

Django is a popular web framework for Python that is designed to help developers build complex, data-driven web applications quickly and efficiently. Django provides a range of features for handling common web development tasks, including URL routing, form handling, database management, and more.

Getting Started with Django

To get started with Django, you first need to install it using pip, the Python package manager. Once you have Django installed, you can create a new Django project using the django-admin startproject command.

```
$ pip install django
$ django-admin startproject myproject
```

This will create a new Django project with the name "myproject". The project directory will contain a number of files and directories that Django uses to manage your application.

Working with Models and Databases

One of the most powerful features of Django is its support for working with databases. Django provides a powerful Object-Relational Mapping (ORM) system that allows you to define your database schema using Python classes.

Here's an example of using the Django ORM to define a simple model:

```python
from django.db import models

class Book(models.Model):
    title = models.CharField(max_length=200)
    author = models.CharField(max_length=200)
    pub_date = models.DateField()

    def __str__(self):
        return self.title
```

In this example, we define a Book model that has three fields: title, author, and pub_date. The __str__ method defines how the object should be represented as a string.

To use the Book model in our application, we need to create a database table for it. We can do this using the migrate command, which creates the necessary database tables based on the models we have defined.

```
$ python manage.py makemigrations
$ python manage.py migrate
```

Working with Views and Templates

In Django, views are Python functions that handle requests and generate responses. Views can use templates to generate HTML pages dynamically.

Here's an example of a simple view that uses a template:

```
from django.shortcuts import render
from .models import Book

def book_list(request):
    books = Book.objects.all()
    return render(request, 'book_list.html', {'books': books})
```

Introduction to Django

Django is a popular web framework for Python that is designed to help developers build complex, data-driven web applications quickly and efficiently. Django provides a range of features for handling common web development tasks, including URL routing, form handling, database management, and more.

Getting Started with Django

To get started with Django, you first need to install it using pip, the Python package manager. Once you have Django installed, you can create a new Django project using the django-admin startproject command.

```
python
Copy code
$ pip install django
$ django-admin startproject myproject
```
This will create a new Django project with the name "myproject". The project directory will contain a number of files and directories that Django uses to manage your application.

Working with Models and Databases

One of the most powerful features of Django is its support for working with databases. Django provides a powerful Object-Relational Mapping (ORM) system that allows you to define your database schema using Python classes.

Here's an example of using the Django ORM to define a simple model:

```python
from django.db import models

class Book(models.Model):
    title = models.CharField(max_length=200)
    author = models.CharField(max_length=200)
    pub_date = models.DateField()

    def __str__(self):
        return self.title
```

In this example, we define a Book model that has three fields: title, author, and pub_date. The __str__ method defines how the object should be represented as a string.

To use the Book model in our application, we need to create a database table for it. We can do this using the migrate command, which creates the necessary database tables based on the models we have defined.

```
$ python manage.py makemigrations
$ python manage.py migrate
```

Working with Views and Templates

In Django, views are Python functions that handle requests and generate responses. Views can use templates to generate HTML pages dynamically.

Here's an example of a simple view that uses a template:

```python
python
Copy code
from django.shortcuts import render
from .models import Book

def book_list(request):
    books = Book.objects.all()
    return render(request, 'book_list.html', {'books': books})
```

In this example, we define a book_list view that retrieves all the books from the database using the Book.objects.all() method. We then pass the list of books to a template called book_list.html using the render function.

Here's an example of a simple template that displays the list of books:

```html
<!DOCTYPE html>
<html>
<head>
    <title>Book List</title>
</head>
<body>
    <h1>Book List</h1>
    <ul>
        {% for book in books %}
            <li>{{ book.title }} by {{ book.author }} (published on {{ book.pub_date }})</li>
        {% endfor %}
    </ul>
</body>
</html>
```

In this template, we use the Django template language to loop over the list of books and display the title, author, and publication date for each book.

Django is a powerful and flexible web framework for Python that provides a range of features for building complex, data-driven web applications. With its support for models, views, templates, and databases, Django makes it easy to create dynamic, interactive web pages that can be used for a variety of purposes. Whether you are building a simple blog or a complex e-commerce site, Django is a great choice for your next web development project.

Using Pyramid for web development

Pyramid is a web framework for Python that is designed to be flexible and easy to use. It provides a range of features for building web applications, including URL routing, templating, database integration, and more.

Getting Started with Pyramid

To get started with Pyramid, you first need to install it using pip, the Python package manager. Once you have Pyramid installed, you can create a new Pyramid project using the pcreate command.

```
$ pip install pyramid
$ pcreate -s starter myproject
```

This will create a new Pyramid project with the name "myproject". The project directory will contain a number of files and directories that Pyramid uses to manage your application.

Working with Views and Templates

In Pyramid, views are Python functions that handle requests and generate responses. Views can use templates to generate HTML pages dynamically.

Here's an example of a simple view that uses a template:

```python
from pyramid.view import view_config
from myproject.models import Book

@view_config(route_name='book_list', renderer='templates/book_list.jinja2')
def book_list(request):
    books = request.dbsession.query(Book).all()
    return {'books': books}
```

In this example, we define a book_list view that retrieves all the books from the database using the request.dbsession.query(Book).all() method. We then pass the list of books to a template called book_list.jinja2 using the @view_config decorator.

Here's an example of a simple template that displays the list of books:

```html
<!DOCTYPE html>
<html>
<head>
```

```
    <title>Book List</title>
</head>
<body>
    <h1>Book List</h1>
    <ul>
        {% for book in books %}
            <li>{{ book.title }} by {{ book.author }} (published on {{ book.pub_date }})</li>
        {% endfor %}
    </ul>
</body>
</html>
```

In this template, we use the Jinja2 template language to loop over the list of books and display the title, author, and publication date for each book.

Working with Models and Databases

Pyramid uses SQLAlchemy, a popular Object-Relational Mapping (ORM) library, for working with databases. To use SQLAlchemy in your Pyramid application, you need to configure a database engine and create a session factory.

Here's an example of how to configure a database engine in Pyramid:

```
from sqlalchemy import create_engine
from sqlalchemy.orm import sessionmaker

def main(global_config, **settings):
    engine = create_engine(settings['sqlalchemy.url'])
    session_factory = sessionmaker(bind=engine)
    return {'dbsession': scoped_session(session_factory)}
```

In this example, we create a database engine using the settings defined in global_config. We then create a session factory and return a dictionary that includes a dbsession key that is bound to a scoped session.

Pyramid is a flexible and easy-to-use web framework for Python that provides a range of features for building web applications. With its support for views, templates, and databases, Pyramid makes it easy to create dynamic, interactive web pages that can be used for a variety of purposes. Whether you are building a simple blog or a complex e-commerce site, Pyramid is a great choice for your next web development project.

Web scraping with Python

Web scraping is a powerful tool that can be used to gather data from websites for a variety of purposes, such as data analysis, research, and content creation. In this text, we will explore the basics of web scraping with Python, including how to use popular libraries like Beautiful Soup and Scrapy to extract data from websites.

What is Web Scraping?

Web scraping refers to the automated process of extracting data from websites. This can be done manually, but it can be time-consuming and error-prone. Web scraping automates this process by using a program to extract data from websites automatically.

There are many different ways to scrape data from websites, but the most common method is to use a program to request the HTML code of a webpage and then parse that code to extract the relevant data. This can be done using Python, which is a popular programming language for web scraping due to its flexibility and ease of use.

Web Scraping Libraries in Python

Python has a number of libraries that can be used for web scraping, including Beautiful Soup, Scrapy, and Requests. In this text, we will focus on Beautiful Soup and Scrapy, which are two of the most popular and widely used libraries for web scraping in Python.

Beautiful Soup

Beautiful Soup is a Python library for pulling data out of HTML and XML files. It creates a parse tree for parsed pages that can be used to extract data from HTML, which is useful for web scraping. Beautiful Soup provides a few simple methods and Pythonic idioms for navigating, searching, and modifying a parse tree, making it a great choice for beginners.

Here is an example of how to use Beautiful Soup to extract the title of a webpage:

```
from bs4 import BeautifulSoup
import requests

url = 'https://www.example.com'
response = requests.get(url)
soup = BeautifulSoup(response.text, 'html.parser')

title = soup.title.string

print(title)
```

In this example, we first import the necessary libraries: BeautifulSoup and requests. We then define the URL of the webpage we want to scrape and use the requests library to make a request for the HTML code of the page. We then use Beautiful Soup to parse the HTML code and extract the title of the page.

Scrapy

Scrapy is a Python web crawling framework that provides a complete toolset for extracting data from websites. It allows you to define a set of rules for how to navigate a website and extract data, making it a powerful tool for web scraping at scale.

Here is an example of how to use Scrapy to scrape data from a webpage:

```
import scrapy

class MySpider(scrapy.Spider):
    name = 'myspider'
    start_urls = ['https://www.example.com']

    def parse(self, response):
        title = response.css('title::text').get()

        yield {
            'title': title,
        }
```

In this example, we define a new Scrapy spider called "MySpider". We set the starting URL of the spider to the website we want to scrape and define a "parse" method that extracts the title of the page using a CSS selector. We then use the "yield" statement to return the extracted data.

Web scraping is a powerful tool for gathering data from websites, and Python provides a number of libraries that make it easy to do. In this text, we explored two of the most popular libraries for web scraping in Python: Beautiful Soup and Scrapy. These libraries provide a range of tools for extracting data from websites, and are great choices for beginners and experts alike.

• Data analysis with Python

Python is one of the most popular programming languages for data analysis due to its flexibility and ease of use. In this text, we will explore the basics of data analysis with Python, including how to use popular libraries like Pandas, NumPy, and Matplotlib to manipulate, analyze, and visualize data.

What is Data Analysis?

Data analysis is the process of inspecting, cleaning, transforming, and modeling data to discover useful information, draw conclusions, and support decision-making. It is a crucial step in many fields, including business, science, engineering, and social sciences.

Python provides a range of tools for data analysis, including libraries that can be used to manipulate, analyze, and visualize data. In this text, we will focus on three popular libraries for data analysis: Pandas, NumPy, and Matplotlib.

Pandas

Pandas is a Python library for data manipulation and analysis. It provides data structures and functions for working with structured data, including tabular data like spreadsheets and databases. Pandas is built on top of NumPy, which makes it fast and efficient for large datasets.

Here is an example of how to use Pandas to read a CSV file and print the first few rows:

```
import pandas as pd

data = pd.read_csv('data.csv')

print(data.head())
```

In this example, we first import the Pandas library and then use the read_csv function to read a CSV file called data.csv. We then use the head function to print the first few rows of the data.

Pandas provides a range of functions for data manipulation and analysis, including filtering, grouping, merging, and aggregation. It also provides powerful tools for data cleaning and handling missing data.

NumPy

NumPy is a Python library for scientific computing that provides a range of functions for working with numerical data. It provides a powerful array object that can be used for efficient computation with large datasets.

Here is an example of how to use NumPy to create an array and perform some basic operations:

```
import numpy as np

data = np.array([1, 2, 3, 4, 5])

print(data.mean())
print(data.max())
```

In this example, we first import the NumPy library and then use the array function to create an array with the values 1 through 5. We then use the mean and max functions to calculate the mean and maximum values of the array.

NumPy provides a range of functions for numerical computation, including linear algebra, Fourier analysis, and random number generation. It also provides functions for working with multidimensional arrays and matrices, which can be useful for image processing, signal processing, and machine learning.

Matplotlib

Matplotlib is a Python library for creating visualizations and plots. It provides a range of functions for creating line plots, scatter plots, bar plots, histograms, and more. Matplotlib can be used for data exploration, communication, and presentation.

Here is an example of how to use Matplotlib to create a simple line plot:

```
import matplotlib.pyplot as plt
import numpy as np

x = np.linspace(0, 10, 100)
y = np.sin(x)

plt.plot(x, y)
plt.show()
```

In this example, we first import the Matplotlib library and the NumPy library. We then use the linspace function from NumPy to create an array of 100 evenly spaced points between 0 and 10. We use the sin function from NumPy to create an array of y-values based on the x-values. We then use the plot function from Matplotlib to create a line plot of the data and the show function to display the plot.

Matplotlib provides a range of functions for creating different types of visualizations, including line plots, scatter plots, bar plots, histograms, heatmaps, and more. It also provides tools for customizing the appearance of plots, including colors, labels, legends, and annotations.

Data Analysis Example

Let's put these libraries to use in a simple data analysis example. Suppose we have a CSV file containing information about customers, including their age, gender, and purchase history. We want to analyze this data to understand the demographics of our customers and their purchasing patterns.

Here is an example of how to use Pandas, NumPy, and Matplotlib to perform some basic analysis:

```python
import pandas as pd
import numpy as np
import matplotlib.pyplot as plt

data = pd.read_csv('customers.csv')

# Calculate the average age of customers
avg_age = data['age'].mean()
print('Average age:', avg_age)

# Create a histogram of customer ages
plt.hist(data['age'], bins=20)
plt.xlabel('Age')
plt.ylabel('Frequency')
plt.show()

# Calculate the total amount spent by male and female customers
male_spending = data[data['gender'] == 'Male']['amount'].sum()
female_spending = data[data['gender'] == 'Female']['amount'].sum()

# Calculate the average amount spent per purchase
avg_spending = data['amount'].mean()
print('Average spending:', avg_spending)

# Create a bar chart of spending by gender
gender_spending = [male_spending, female_spending]
labels = ['Male', 'Female']
plt.bar(labels, gender_spending)
plt.xlabel('Gender')
plt.ylabel('Total Spending')
plt.show()
```

In this example, we first use Pandas to read a CSV file called customers.csv. We then calculate the average age of customers and create a histogram of customer ages using Matplotlib. We also calculate the total amount spent by male and female customers and create a bar chart of spending by gender using Matplotlib.

This is just a simple example, but it illustrates how Pandas, NumPy, and Matplotlib can be used together to perform data analysis tasks. With these tools, you can manipulate, analyze, and visualize data in a flexible and efficient way, making it easier to draw insights and make decisions based on data.

Introduction to data analysis libraries (NumPy, Pandas, Matplotlib, etc.)

4Data analysis is the process of inspecting, cleaning, transforming, and modeling data to discover useful information, draw conclusions, and support decision-making. Python is a powerful programming language for data analysis, with a rich ecosystem of libraries and tools that make it easier to work with data.

We will introduce some of the most commonly used data analysis libraries in Python, including NumPy, Pandas, and Matplotlib.

NumPy
NumPy is a fundamental library for numerical computing in Python. It provides a powerful array object, which is similar to a list or tuple but optimized for numerical operations. NumPy arrays can be used to store and manipulate large sets of data efficiently, and they support a wide range of mathematical operations.

Here is an example of how to create a NumPy array and perform some basic operations:

import numpy as np

```
# Create a NumPy array from a list
arr = np.array([1, 2, 3, 4, 5])

# Perform basic operations on the array
print('Array:', arr)
print('Sum:', arr.sum())
print('Mean:', arr.mean())
print('Standard deviation:', arr.std())
```

In this example, we create a NumPy array from a list of integers, and then perform some basic operations on the array, including calculating the sum, mean, and standard deviation.

NumPy also provides a range of other functions for working with arrays, including mathematical functions, statistical functions, and linear algebra functions.

Pandas
Pandas is a library for data manipulation and analysis in Python. It provides powerful data structures for working with structured data, including the Series and DataFrame objects.

Here is an example of how to use Pandas to read a CSV file and perform some basic operations:

```python
import pandas as pd

# Read a CSV file into a DataFrame
data = pd.read_csv('data.csv')

# Display the first few rows of the DataFrame
print('Head:')
print(data.head())

# Display basic statistics about the DataFrame
print('Describe:')
print(data.describe())

# Filter the DataFrame by a condition
print('Filtered data:')
print(data[data['age'] > 30])
```

In this example, we use Pandas to read a CSV file called data.csv into a DataFrame, which is a two-dimensional table of data. We then display the first few rows of the DataFrame, calculate basic statistics about the data, and filter the DataFrame based on a condition.

Pandas provides a range of functions for working with DataFrames and Series, including filtering, sorting, grouping, merging, and more.

Matplotlib
Matplotlib is a library for creating static, animated, and interactive visualizations in Python. It provides a range of functions for creating different types of plots, including line plots, scatter plots, bar plots, histograms, and more.

Here is an example of how to use Matplotlib to create a simple line plot:

```python
import matplotlib.pyplot as plt

# Create some data for the plot
x = [1, 2, 3, 4, 5]
y = [1, 4, 9, 16, 25]

# Create a line plot of the data
plt.plot(x, y)

# Add labels and a title to the plot
plt.xlabel('X')
plt.ylabel('Y')
```

```
plt.title('My Plot')

# Display the plot
plt.show()
```

In this example, we create some data for a line plot, and then use Matplotlib to create the plot, add labels and a title, and display the plot.

Matplotlib provides a range of customization options for plots, including colors, labels, legends, and annotations.

NumPy, Pandas, and Matplotlib are just a few of the many libraries available for data analysis in Python. By using these libraries, you can efficiently manipulate and visualize large sets of data, making it easier to draw insights and make informed decisions.

In addition to these libraries, there are many others that are commonly used in data analysis, including SciPy, Seaborn, Scikit-learn, and more. Each library has its own strengths and weaknesses, and choosing the right library for a specific task can make a significant difference in the quality and efficiency of your data analysis.

Overall, Python has become a go-to language for data analysis due to its powerful libraries and tools. Whether you are working with large datasets or simply exploring small data samples, these libraries can help streamline your workflow and make data analysis more accessible to a wider range of users.

Data visualization with Matplotlib

Data visualization is an essential part of data analysis that helps to uncover insights and trends in data. Matplotlib is a popular Python library for creating static, animated, and interactive visualizations that are essential in data visualization.

We'll discuss how to use Matplotlib to create various types of visualizations, including line plots, scatter plots, bar plots, and histograms.

Line Plots

Line plots are one of the most basic types of visualization that is useful in data analysis. They are useful for visualizing trends and patterns in data. Here's an example of how to create a simple line plot using Matplotlib:

```python
import matplotlib.pyplot as plt

# Create some data for the plot
x = [1, 2, 3, 4, 5]
y = [1, 4, 9, 16, 25]

# Create a line plot of the data
plt.plot(x, y)

# Add labels and a title to the plot
plt.xlabel('X')
plt.ylabel('Y')
plt.title('My Plot')

# Display the plot
plt.show()
```

In this example, we create some data for a line plot, and then use Matplotlib to create the plot, add labels and a title, and display the plot.

Scatter Plots

Scatter plots are another common type of visualization that is useful for visualizing relationships between two variables. Here's an example of how to create a simple scatter plot using Matplotlib:

```python
import matplotlib.pyplot as plt

# Create some data for the plot
x = [1, 2, 3, 4, 5]
```

```
y = [1, 4, 9, 16, 25]

# Create a scatter plot of the data
plt.scatter(x, y)

# Add labels and a title to the plot
plt.xlabel('X')
plt.ylabel('Y')
plt.title('My Scatter Plot')

# Display the plot
plt.show()
```

In this example, we create some data for a scatter plot, and then use Matplotlib to create the plot, add labels and a title, and display the plot.

Bar Plots

Bar plots are another useful type of visualization that is useful for visualizing categorical data. Here's an example of how to create a simple bar plot using Matplotlib:

```
import matplotlib.pyplot as plt

# Create some data for the plot
x = ['A', 'B', 'C', 'D', 'E']
y = [1, 4, 9, 16, 25]

# Create a bar plot of the data
plt.bar(x, y)

# Add labels and a title to the plot
plt.xlabel('X')
plt.ylabel('Y')
plt.title('My Bar Plot')

# Display the plot
plt.show()
```

In this example, we create some data for a bar plot, and then use Matplotlib to create the plot, add labels and a title, and display the plot.

Histograms

Histograms are another useful type of visualization that is useful for visualizing the distribution of data. Here's an example of how to create a simple histogram using Matplotlib:

```
import matplotlib.pyplot as plt
import numpy as np

# Create some data for the histogram
data = np.random.randn(1000)

# Create a histogram of the data
plt.hist(data, bins=30)

# Add labels and a title to the plot
plt.xlabel('Data')
plt.ylabel('Frequency')
plt.title('My Histogram')

# Display the plot
plt.show()
```

In this example, we create some data for a histogram, and then use Matplotlib to create the plot, add labels and a title, and display the plot.

Customizing Plots

Matplotlib provides a wide range of customization options that allow you to create professional-looking plots that effectively communicate your data. You can customize everything from the color and style of the plot to the font size and axis labels. Here are a few examples of how to customize plots using Matplotlib:

```
import matplotlib.pyplot as plt

# Create some data for the plot
x = [1, 2, 3, 4, 5]
y = [1, 4, 9, 16, 25]

# Create a line plot of the data
plt.plot(x, y, color='red', linestyle='dashed', linewidth=2)

# Add labels and a title to the plot
plt.xlabel('X', fontsize=14)
plt.ylabel('Y', fontsize=14)
plt.title('My Plot', fontsize=16)

# Display the plot
plt.show()
```

In this example, we create a line plot and customize the color, linestyle, and linewidth of the plot. We also increase the font size of the labels and title.

```
import matplotlib.pyplot as plt

# Create some data for the plot
x = ['A', 'B', 'C', 'D', 'E']
y = [1, 4, 9, 16, 25]

# Create a bar plot of the data
plt.bar(x, y, color=['red', 'green', 'blue', 'yellow', 'purple'])

# Add labels and a title to the plot
plt.xlabel('X', fontsize=14)
plt.ylabel('Y', fontsize=14)
plt.title('My Bar Plot', fontsize=16)

# Display the plot
plt.show()
```

In this example, we create a bar plot and customize the color of each bar.

We have discussed how to use Matplotlib to create various types of visualizations, including line plots, scatter plots, bar plots, and histograms. We have also explored how to customize plots to make them more visually appealing and effective in communicating data. Matplotlib is a powerful library that is essential in data visualization, and by mastering it, you can create professional-looking plots that effectively communicate your data.

• Machine learning with Python

Machine learning is a field of study that focuses on creating algorithms that can learn from data to make predictions or decisions. In this chapter, we will introduce the fundamental concepts of machine learning and explore some of the popular machine learning algorithms.

Chapter 1: What is Machine Learning?

Machine learning is a subfield of artificial intelligence that deals with the development of algorithms that can learn from data. The goal of machine learning is to create models that can make predictions or decisions based on input data without being explicitly programmed to do so.

Types of Machine Learning

There are three main types of machine learning: supervised learning, unsupervised learning, and reinforcement learning.

Supervised Learning

Supervised learning is a type of machine learning where the algorithm learns from labeled data. The labeled data consists of input features and their corresponding output labels. The goal of supervised learning is to create a model that can accurately predict the output labels for new input data.

```python
from sklearn.datasets import load_iris
from sklearn.tree import DecisionTreeClassifier
from sklearn.model_selection import train_test_split

# Load the Iris dataset
iris = load_iris()

# Split the dataset into training and testing sets
X_train, X_test, y_train, y_test = train_test_split(iris.data, iris.target, test_size=0.3, random_state=42)

# Create a Decision Tree classifier and train it on the training data
clf = DecisionTreeClassifier()
clf.fit(X_train, y_train)

# Test the model on the testing data
accuracy = clf.score(X_test, y_test)
print("Accuracy:", accuracy)
```

In this example, we use the Iris dataset to train a Decision Tree classifier using supervised learning. We split the dataset into training and testing sets and then train the classifier on the training data. Finally, we test the accuracy of the model on the testing data.

Unsupervised Learning
Unsupervised learning is a type of machine learning where the algorithm learns from unlabeled data. The goal of unsupervised learning is to find patterns or structure in the data without any prior knowledge of the output labels.

```python
from sklearn.datasets import load_iris
from sklearn.cluster import KMeans

# Load the Iris dataset
iris = load_iris()

# Create a KMeans clustering model and train it on the data
kmeans = KMeans(n_clusters=3, random_state=42)
kmeans.fit(iris.data)

# Get the predicted labels for each data point
labels = kmeans.predict(iris.data)

# Print the predicted labels
print("Predicted Labels:", labels)
```

In this example, we use the Iris dataset to perform clustering using unsupervised learning. We create a KMeans clustering model and train it on the data. Finally, we get the predicted labels for each data point.

Reinforcement Learning
Reinforcement learning is a type of machine learning where the algorithm learns by interacting with an environment. The goal of reinforcement learning is to learn a policy that maximizes a reward signal.

Popular Machine Learning Algorithms
There are many machine learning algorithms, each with its own strengths and weaknesses. In this section, we will introduce some of the popular machine learning algorithms.

Linear Regression
Linear regression is a supervised learning algorithm used to predict a continuous output variable. The algorithm learns a linear relationship between the input features and the output variable.

```
import numpy as np
from sklearn.linear_model import LinearRegression

# Create some data for the model
X = np.array([[1], [2], [3], [4], [5]])
y = np.array([2, 4, 6, 8, 10])

# Create a Linear Regression model and train it on the data

model = LinearRegression()
model.fit(X, y)

Predict the output variable for a new input feature
y_pred = model.predict([[6]])

Print the predicted output variable
print("Predicted Output Variable:", y_pred)
```

In this example, we create some data and use linear regression to predict the output variable based on the input feature. We train the model on the data and then use it to predict the output variable for a new input feature.

Logistic Regression

Logistic regression is a supervised learning algorithm used for binary classification. The algorithm learns a linear relationship between the input features and the probability of the binary output variable.

```
import numpy as np
from sklearn.linear_model import LogisticRegression

# Create some data for the model
X = np.array([[1], [2], [3], [4], [5]])
y = np.array([0, 0, 1, 1, 1])

# Create a Logistic Regression model and train it on the data
model = LogisticRegression()
model.fit(X, y)

# Predict the output variable for a new input feature
y_pred = model.predict([[6]])

# Print the predicted output variable
print("Predicted Output Variable:", y_pred)
```

In this example, we create some data and use logistic regression to predict the binary output variable based on the input feature. We train the model on the data and then use it to predict the output variable for a new input feature.

Decision Trees

Decision trees are supervised learning algorithms used for classification and regression. The algorithm creates a tree-like model of decisions and their possible consequences based on the input features.

```python
from sklearn.datasets import load_iris
from sklearn.tree import DecisionTreeClassifier
from sklearn.model_selection import train_test_split

# Load the Iris dataset
iris = load_iris()

# Split the dataset into training and testing sets
X_train, X_test, y_train, y_test = train_test_split(iris.data, iris.target, test_size=0.3, random_state=42)

# Create a Decision Tree classifier and train it on the training data
clf = DecisionTreeClassifier()
clf.fit(X_train, y_train)

# Test the model on the testing data
accuracy = clf.score(X_test, y_test)
print("Accuracy:", accuracy)
```

In this example, we use the Iris dataset to train a Decision Tree classifier using supervised learning. We split the dataset into training and testing sets and then train the classifier on the training data. Finally, we test the accuracy of the model on the testing data.

Chapter 2: Data Preprocessing

Before we can apply machine learning algorithms to our data, we need to preprocess it to ensure that it is in a suitable format. In this chapter, we will explore some common data preprocessing techniques.

Data Cleaning
Data cleaning is the process of removing or correcting any errors or inconsistencies in the data. This can include removing missing values, correcting invalid values, and removing outliers.

```
import pandas as pd

# Load the data
data = pd.read_csv("data.csv")

# Remove any rows with missing values
data = data.dropna()

# Correct any invalid values
data["age"] = data["age"].apply(lambda x: x if x > 0 else 30)

# Remove any outliers
data = data[data["height"] < 7]
```

In this example, we load some data from a CSV file and perform data cleaning. We remove any rows with missing values, correct any invalid values in the "age" column, and remove any outliers in the "height" column.

Data Transformation
Data transformation is the process of converting the data into a suitable format for machine learning algorithms. This can include scaling the data , encoding categorical variables, and creating new features.

Scaling
Scaling is the process of transforming the data to a similar scale, typically between 0 and 1 or -1 and 1. This is important because machine learning algorithms may not perform well when the input features are on different scales.

```
from sklearn.preprocessing import MinMaxScaler

# Load the data
data = pd.read_csv("data.csv")

# Scale the data
scaler = MinMaxScaler()
scaled_data = scaler.fit_transform(data)
```

In this example, we load some data from a CSV file and scale it using the MinMaxScaler from the scikit-learn library.

Encoding Categorical Variables
Categorical variables are variables that can take on a limited number of values, such as "red", "green", or "blue". These variables need to be encoded as numbers before they can be used in machine learning algorithms.

```
import pandas as pd
from sklearn.preprocessing import LabelEncoder

# Load the data
data = pd.read_csv("data.csv")

# Encode the categorical variable
encoder = LabelEncoder()
data["color"] = encoder.fit_transform(data["color"])
```

In this example, we load some data from a CSV file and encode the categorical variable "color" using the LabelEncoder from the scikit-learn library.

Creating New Features
New features can be created from the existing features in the data. This can be done to capture more information or to simplify the input features.

```
import pandas as pd

# Load the data
data = pd.read_csv("data.csv")

# Create a new feature
data["age_group"] = pd.cut(data["age"], bins=[0, 18, 30, 50, 100], labels=["child", "young adult", "middle-aged", "elderly"])
```

In this example, we load some data from a CSV file and create a new feature "age_group" based on the "age" feature. We use the cut function from the pandas library to split the "age" feature into four bins and label them accordingly.

Chapter 3: Model Selection and Evaluation

Once we have preprocessed our data, we can start applying machine learning algorithms to it. However, we need to ensure that we select the right algorithm for our problem and evaluate its performance.

Model Selection
Model selection is the process of choosing the best algorithm for our problem. This can be done by comparing the performance of multiple algorithms on our data.

```
from sklearn.model_selection import cross_val_score
from sklearn.linear_model import LinearRegression, LogisticRegression
from sklearn.tree import DecisionTreeClassifier
```

```
# Load the data
data = pd.read_csv("data.csv")

# Split the data into input features and output variables
X = data.drop("target", axis=1)
y = data["target"]

# Compare the performance of multiple algorithms using cross-validation
models = [
    ("Linear Regression", LinearRegression()),
    ("Logistic Regression", LogisticRegression()),
    ("Decision Tree Classifier", DecisionTreeClassifier())
]

for name, model in models:
    scores = cross_val_score(model, X, y, cv=5)
    print(f"{name}: {scores.mean()}")
```

In this example, we load some data from a CSV file and split it into input features and output variables. We then compare the performance of three different algorithms using cross-validation.

Model Evaluation
Model evaluation is the process of measuring the performance of our selected algorithm. This can be done using various metrics, such as accuracy, precision, recall, and F1 score.

```
from sklearn.metrics import accuracy_score, precision_score, recall_score, f1_score
from sklearn.linear_model import LogisticRegression

# Load the data
data = pd.read_csv("data.csv")

Split the data into input features and output variables
X = data.drop("target", axis=1)
y = data["target"]

Train a logistic regression model
model = LogisticRegression()
model.fit(X, y)

Evaluate the model using various metrics
y_pred = model.predict(X)
accuracy = accuracy_score(y, y_pred)
precision = precision_score(y, y_pred)
recall = recall_score(y, y_pred)
f1 = f1_score(y, y_pred)

print(f"Accuracy: {accuracy}")
print(f"Precision: {precision}")
```

```
print(f"Recall: {recall}")
print(f"F1 Score: {f1}")
```

In this example, we load some data from a CSV file and split it into input features and output variables. We then train a logistic regression model on the data and evaluate its performance using various metrics.

Chapter 4: Supervised Learning Algorithms

Supervised learning algorithms are machine learning algorithms that learn from labeled data. In other words, the output variable is known for each input example.

Linear Regression

Linear regression is a supervised learning algorithm for predicting a continuous output variable. It assumes a linear relationship between the input features and the output variable.

```
from sklearn.linear_model import LinearRegression
import pandas as pd

# Load the data
data = pd.read_csv("data.csv")

# Split the data into input features and output variables
X = data.drop("target", axis=1)
y = data["target"]

# Train a linear regression model
model = LinearRegression()
model.fit(X, y)

# Predict the output variable for new input examples
y_pred = model.predict(X)
```

In this example, we load some data from a CSV file and split it into input features and output variables. We then train a linear regression model on the data and use it to predict the output variable for new input examples.

Logistic Regression
Logistic regression is a supervised learning algorithm for predicting a binary output variable. It assumes a linear relationship between the input features and the log-odds of the output variable.

```
from sklearn.linear_model import LogisticRegression
import pandas as pd

# Load the data
data = pd.read_csv("data.csv")

# Split the data into input features and output variables
X = data.drop("target", axis=1)
y = data["target"]

# Train a logistic regression model
model = LogisticRegression()
model.fit(X, y)

# Predict the output variable for new input examples
y_pred = model.predict(X)
```

In this example, we load some data from a CSV file and split it into input features and output variables. We then train a logistic regression model on the data and use it to predict the output variable for new input examples.

Decision Trees

Decision trees are supervised learning algorithms for predicting a discrete output variable. They create a tree-like model of decisions and their possible consequences.

```
from sklearn.tree import DecisionTreeClassifier
import pandas as pd

# Load the data
data = pd.read_csv("data.csv")

# Split the data into input features and output variables
X = data.drop("target", axis=1)
y = data["target"]

# Train a decision tree classifier
model = DecisionTreeClassifier()
model.fit(X, y)

# Predict the output variable for new input examples
y_pred = model.predict(X)
```

In this example, we load some data from a CSV file and split it into input features and output variables. We then train a decision tree classifier on the data and use it to predict the output variable for new input examples.

Chapter 5: Unsupervised Learning Algorithms

Unsupervised learning algorithms are machine learning algorithms that learn from unlabeled data. In other words, the output variable is not known for each input example.

K-Means Clustering

K-means clustering is an unsupervised learning algorithm for grouping similar input examples into clusters. It assumes that each cluster is represented by its centroid, which is the average of all input examples in the cluster.

```python
from sklearn.cluster import KMeans
import pandas as pd

# Load the data
data = pd.read_csv("data.csv")

# Train a k-means clustering model
model = KMeans(n_clusters=2)
model.fit(data)

# Predict the cluster labels for new input examples
labels = model.predict(data)
```

In this example, we load some data from a CSV file and train a k-means clustering model on the data. We then use the model to predict the cluster labels for new input examples.

Principal Component Analysis

Principal component analysis (PCA) is an unsupervised learning algorithm for reducing the dimensionality of input data. It finds the principal components of the data, which are linear combinations of the input features that explain the most variance in the data.

```python
from sklearn.decomposition import PCA
import pandas as pd

# Load the data
data = pd.read_csv("data.csv")

# Apply PCA to the data
pca = PCA(n_components=2)
X_pca = pca.fit_transform(data)

# Visualize the transformed data
import matplotlib.pyplot as plt
plt.scatter(X_pca[:, 0], X_pca[:, 1])
```

```
plt.show()
```

In this example, we load some data from a CSV file and apply PCA to the data to reduce its dimensionality. We then visualize the transformed data using a scatter plot.

Chapter 6: Deep Learning

Deep learning is a subset of machine learning that uses neural networks with multiple layers to learn from data.

Artificial Neural Networks
Artificial neural networks (ANNs) are a type of neural network that consists of interconnected nodes, or neurons, that process input data and generate output predictions.

```python
from keras.models import Sequential
from keras.layers import Dense
import pandas as pd

# Load the data
data = pd.read_csv("data.csv")

# Split the data into input features and output variables
X = data.drop("target", axis=1)
y = data["target"]

# Define an artificial neural network model
model = Sequential()
model.add(Dense(10, input_dim=X.shape[1], activation="relu"))
model.add(Dense(1, activation="sigmoid"))

# Compile the model
model.compile(loss="binary_crossentropy", optimizer="adam", metrics=["accuracy"])

# Train the model
model.fit(X, y, epochs=10, batch_size=32)

# Evaluate the model on the test data
_, accuracy = model.evaluate(X, y)
print(f"Accuracy: {accuracy}")
```

In this example, we load some data from a CSV file and split it into input features and output variables. We then define an artificial neural network model using the Keras library, compile it, and train it on the data. Finally, we evaluate the model on the test data and print its accuracy.

In this book, we have covered the basics of machine learning and some of the most commonly used algorithms and techniques in the field. We have also provided practical examples of how to implement these algorithms using Python code and popular machine learning libraries like scikit-learn and Keras.

Machine learning is a vast and rapidly evolving field, and there is always more to learn. We hope that this book has provided you with a solid foundation for further exploration and experimentation with machine learning. Happy learning!

Introduction to machine learning libraries (Scikit-learn, TensorFlow, Keras, etc.)

Machine Learning (ML) is an exciting field that has seen a rapid rise in popularity over the past few years. ML algorithms have been used to solve a wide range of problems, from image recognition and natural language processing to fraud detection and predictive analytics. In this article, we will provide an overview of some of the most popular ML libraries used by developers and data scientists today, including Scikit-learn, TensorFlow, Keras, and more.

Scikit-learn

Scikit-learn is a Python library that provides a wide range of ML algorithms, including classification, regression, clustering, and dimensionality reduction. It is built on top of other popular Python libraries, including NumPy, SciPy, and Matplotlib, and provides a simple and easy-to-use API for building and training ML models. Scikit-learn also provides a variety of tools for model selection, data preprocessing, and feature extraction, making it an ideal choice for both beginners and experienced ML practitioners.

Here's an example of using Scikit-learn to train a simple linear regression model:

```
from sklearn.linear_model import LinearRegression
from sklearn.datasets import load_boston

# Load the Boston housing dataset
boston = load_boston()

# Split the data into training and testing sets
X_train, X_test, y_train, y_test = train_test_split(boston.data, boston.target, test_size=0.2, random_state=42)

# Create a Linear Regression model and fit it to the training data
model = LinearRegression()
model.fit(X_train, y_train)

# Evaluate the model on the testing data
score = model.score(X_test, y_test)
print(f"Model score: {score}")
```

TensorFlow

TensorFlow is an open-source ML library developed by Google that is widely used for building deep neural networks. It provides a flexible and scalable platform for developing ML models, from small experiments to large-scale production systems. TensorFlow also provides a rich set of APIs for building and training ML models, including support for distributed training and model deployment.

Here's an example of using TensorFlow to train a simple neural network for image classification:

```
import tensorflow as tf
from tensorflow import keras
from tensorflow.keras import layers

# Load the MNIST dataset
(x_train, y_train), (x_test, y_test) = keras.datasets.mnist.load_data()

# Normalize the pixel values to between 0 and 1
x_train = x_train.astype("float32") / 255
x_test = x_test.astype("float32") / 255

# Create a simple neural network model
model = keras.Sequential(
    [
        keras.Input(shape=(28, 28)),
        layers.Flatten(),
        layers.Dense(128, activation="relu"),
        layers.Dense(10),
    ]
)

# Compile the model with the appropriate loss function and optimizer
model.compile(loss=keras.losses.SparseCategoricalCrossentropy(from_logits=True),
optimizer=keras.optimizers.Adam(lr=0.001), metrics=["accuracy"])

# Train the model on the training data
model.fit(x_train, y_train, batch_size=32, epochs=5, validation_split=0.1)

# Evaluate the model on the testing data
score = model.evaluate(x_test, y_test, verbose=0)
print(f"Model score: {score[1]}")
```

Keras

Keras is a high-level ML library that provides a simple and easy-to-use API for building and training ML models. It is built on top of TensorFlow and provides a simplified interface for building and training neural networks. Keras also provides a variety of pre-trained models that can be used for tasks such as image classification, object detection.

Here's an example of using Keras to train a simple convolutional neural network (CNN) for image classification:

```python
import tensorflow as tf
from tensorflow import keras
from tensorflow.keras import layers

# Load the CIFAR-10 dataset
(x_train, y_train), (x_test, y_test) = keras.datasets.cifar10.load_data()

# Normalize the pixel values to between 0 and 1
x_train = x_train.astype("float32") / 255
x_test = x_test.astype("float32") / 255

# Define the CNN architecture
model = keras.Sequential(
    [
        layers.Conv2D(32, (3, 3), activation="relu", input_shape=(32, 32, 3)),
        layers.MaxPooling2D((2, 2)),
        layers.Conv2D(64, (3, 3), activation="relu"),
        layers.MaxPooling2D((2, 2)),
        layers.Flatten(),
        layers.Dense(64, activation="relu"),
        layers.Dense(10),
    ]
)

# Compile the model with the appropriate loss function and optimizer
model.compile(loss=keras.losses.SparseCategoricalCrossentropy(from_logits=True),
optimizer=keras.optimizers.Adam(lr=0.001), metrics=["accuracy"])

# Train the model on the training data
model.fit(x_train, y_train, batch_size=32, epochs=5, validation_split=0.1)

# Evaluate the model on the testing data
score = model.evaluate(x_test, y_test, verbose=0)
print(f"Model score: {score[1]}")
```

Other ML Libraries

In addition to Scikit-learn, TensorFlow, and Keras, there are many other ML libraries available for Python. Some of these include PyTorch, MXNet, Theano, and Caffe. Each of these libraries has its own strengths and weaknesses, and the choice of which library to use will depend on the specific needs of your project.

Machine learning libraries provide a powerful set of tools for building and training ML models. Whether you are a beginner or an experienced data scientist, there are many libraries available that can help you to quickly build and deploy ML models. In this article, we have provided an overview of some of the most popular ML libraries used today, including Scikit-learn,

TensorFlow, Keras, and more. We hope that this article has been helpful in getting you started on your journey to becoming an ML practitioner.

Supervised learning in Python

Supervised learning is a type of machine learning where an algorithm learns to map input data to output labels based on a labeled training dataset. In this article, we will explore how to implement supervised learning in Python using various machine learning libraries.

Loading Data

Before we can begin training our models, we first need to load our data. In supervised learning, we have a dataset that is split into two parts: the training set and the test set. The training set is used to train our model, while the test set is used to evaluate the performance of our model on new, unseen data.

Here's an example of loading the iris dataset from Scikit-learn:

```
from sklearn.datasets import load_iris

iris = load_iris()
X, y = iris.data, iris.target
```

Splitting Data

Once we have loaded our data, we need to split it into training and test sets. This can be done using Scikit-learn's train_test_split function:

Choosing a Model

Next, we need to choose a model to train on our data. Scikit-learn provides a wide range of models for supervised learning, including linear regression, logistic regression, decision trees, and more. Here's an example of training a linear regression model:

```
from sklearn.linear_model import LinearRegression

model = LinearRegression()
model.fit(X_train, y_train)
```

Evaluating the Model

Once we have trained our model, we need to evaluate its performance on the test set. Scikit-learn provides a range of metrics for evaluating the performance of a supervised learning model, including accuracy, precision, recall, and F1 score. Here's an example of calculating the accuracy of our linear regression model:

```
from sklearn.metrics import accuracy_score

y_pred = model.predict(X_test)
accuracy = accuracy_score(y_test, y_pred)
```

Hyperparameter Tuning

In order to improve the performance of our model, we may need to tune its hyperparameters. Hyperparameters are values that are set before training the model and affect the model's learning process. Scikit-learn provides a range of tools for hyperparameter tuning, including grid search and randomized search. Here's an example of using grid search to tune the hyperparameters of a decision tree classifier:

```
from sklearn.tree import DecisionTreeClassifier
from sklearn.model_selection import GridSearchCV

params = {
    "max_depth": [2, 4, 6, 8],
    "min_samples_split": [2, 4, 8, 16],
}

model = DecisionTreeClassifier()
grid_search = GridSearchCV(model, params, cv=5)
grid_search.fit(X_train, y_train)

best_model = grid_search.best_estimator_
```

Supervised learning is a powerful technique for building predictive models. In this article, we have explored how to implement supervised learning in Python using Scikit-learn. We have covered loading data, splitting data, choosing a model, evaluating the model, and hyperparameter tuning. By following these steps, you can build powerful supervised learning models in Python to solve a wide range of real-world problems.

Unsupervised learning in Python

Unsupervised learning is a type of machine learning where the algorithm learns to identify patterns in data without any predefined labels. In this article, we will explore how to implement unsupervised learning in Python using various machine learning libraries.

Loading Data

Before we can begin training our models, we first need to load our data. In unsupervised learning, we have a dataset that does not have any predefined labels. Here's an example of loading the iris dataset from Scikit-learn:

```
from sklearn.datasets import load_iris

iris = load_iris()
X = iris.data
```

Preprocessing Data

Once we have loaded our data, we need to preprocess it before we can train our models. This can include scaling the data, handling missing values, and more. Here's an example of scaling the data using Scikit-learn's StandardScaler:

```
from sklearn.preprocessing import StandardScaler

scaler = StandardScaler()
X_scaled = scaler.fit_transform(X)
```

Clustering

Clustering is a common unsupervised learning technique that involves grouping similar data points together. Scikit-learn provides a wide range of clustering algorithms, including K-means, DBSCAN, and more. Here's an example of clustering the iris dataset using K-means:

```
from sklearn.cluster import KMeans

kmeans = KMeans(n_clusters=3)
kmeans.fit(X_scaled)
```

Dimensionality Reduction

Dimensionality reduction is another common unsupervised learning technique that involves reducing the number of features in a dataset while preserving as much information as possible. Scikit-learn provides a range of dimensionality reduction algorithms, including Principal Component Analysis (PCA), t-SNE, and more. Here's an example of performing PCA on the iris dataset:

```
from sklearn.decomposition import PCA

pca = PCA(n_components=2)
X_pca = pca.fit_transform(X_scaled)
```

Anomaly Detection

Anomaly detection is another unsupervised learning technique that involves identifying data points that are significantly different from the rest of the data. Scikit-learn provides a range of anomaly detection algorithms, including Local Outlier Factor (LOF), Isolation Forest, and more. Here's an example of performing anomaly detection on the iris dataset using LOF:

```
from sklearn.neighbors import LocalOutlierFactor

lof = LocalOutlierFactor()
y_pred = lof.fit_predict(X_scaled)
```

Unsupervised learning is a powerful technique for identifying patterns in data without predefined labels. In this article, we have explored how to implement unsupervised learning in Python using Scikit-learn. We have covered loading data, preprocessing data, clustering, dimensionality reduction, and anomaly detection. By following these steps, you can build powerful unsupervised learning models in Python to solve a wide range of real-world problems.

Natural Language Processing (NLP) with Python

Natural Language Processing (NLP) is an exciting field of computer science that involves processing human language using computers. Python is a powerful programming language that is widely used in NLP because of its simplicity and versatility.

One of the fundamental tasks in NLP is tokenization, which involves breaking a text into smaller units such as words, phrases, or sentences. In Python, we can use the Natural Language Toolkit (NLTK) library to tokenize text. Here is an example of how to tokenize a sentence using NLTK:

```
import nltk
nltk.download('punkt')

sentence = "The quick brown fox jumps over the lazy dog."
tokens = nltk.word_tokenize(sentence)
print(tokens)
```

This code will output the following tokens:

['The', 'quick', 'brown', 'fox', 'jumps', 'over', 'the', 'lazy', 'dog', '.']

Another important task in NLP is part-of-speech (POS) tagging, which involves assigning a grammatical category to each word in a sentence, such as noun, verb, adjective, etc. In Python, we can use NLTK to perform POS tagging. Here is an example:

```
import nltk
nltk.download('averaged_perceptron_tagger')

sentence = "The quick brown fox jumps over the lazy dog."
tokens = nltk.word_tokenize(sentence)
pos_tags = nltk.pos_tag(tokens)
print(pos_tags)
```

This code will output the following POS tags:

NLP also involves tasks such as named entity recognition, sentiment analysis, and text classification. Python has many libraries and tools available for these tasks, such as spaCy, TextBlob, and scikit-learn.

In conclusion, Python is an excellent choice for NLP because of its ease of use and the availability of many powerful libraries and tools. With Python, you can perform a wide range of NLP tasks and analyze human language in new and exciting ways.

Sentiment analysis with Python

Sentiment analysis is a popular application of Natural Language Processing (NLP) that involves identifying the emotional tone or attitude expressed in a piece of text. Python provides many powerful tools and libraries for performing sentiment analysis on textual data.

Preprocessing the Data
The first step in performing sentiment analysis is to preprocess the data. This involves removing any noise and irrelevant data from the text. Noise can include things like punctuation, special characters, and stop words, which are words that do not carry much meaning on their own, such as "the" or "a". Python provides several libraries for preprocessing text data, such as NLTK and spaCy.

Here is an example of how to preprocess a sentence using NLTK:

```
import nltk
nltk.download('stopwords')
nltk.download('punkt')

from nltk.corpus import stopwords
from nltk.tokenize import word_tokenize

sentence = "I really hate it when my computer crashes."
stop_words = set(stopwords.words('english'))

tokens = word_tokenize(sentence)
filtered_sentence = [w for w in tokens if not w.lower() in stop_words]

print(filtered_sentence)
```

This code will output the following filtered sentence:

['really', 'hate', 'computer', 'crashes', '.']

Building a Sentiment Analysis Model

Once the data has been preprocessed, the next step is to build a model for sentiment analysis. There are many different algorithms and techniques that can be used for sentiment analysis, such as Naive Bayes, Support Vector Machines (SVM), and Recurrent Neural Networks (RNN). In Python, scikit-learn is a popular library for building machine learning models, including models for sentiment analysis.

Here is an example of how to train a Naive Bayes classifier for sentiment analysis using scikit-learn:

```
import pandas as pd
from sklearn.naive_bayes import MultinomialNB
from sklearn.feature_extraction.text import CountVectorizer
from sklearn.metrics import accuracy_score

# Load the dataset
data = pd.read_csv('sentiment_data.csv')

# Preprocess the text data
stop_words = set(stopwords.words('english'))
vectorizer = CountVectorizer(stop_words=stop_words)
X = vectorizer.fit_transform(data['text'])

# Train the classifier
y = data['sentiment']
clf = MultinomialNB()
clf.fit(X, y)

# Test the classifier
test_data = ['I love this product!', 'This movie was terrible.']
X_test = vectorizer.transform(test_data)
y_pred = clf.predict(X_test)
print(y_pred)
```

This code will output the predicted sentiment for the two test sentences:

```
['positive' 'negative']
```

Evaluating the Model

Finally, it is important to evaluate the performance of the sentiment analysis model. This can be done by comparing the predicted sentiment with the actual sentiment for a set of test data. In Python, scikit-learn provides many metrics for evaluating classification models, such as accuracy, precision, recall, and F1 score.

Here is an example of how to evaluate the Naive Bayes classifier using scikit-learn:

```
from sklearn.metrics import classification_report

# Load the test data
test_data = pd.read_csv('sentiment_test.csv')

# Preprocess the text data
X_test = vectorizer.transform(test_data['text'])
```

```
# Test the classifier
y_test = test_data['sentiment']
y_pred = clf.predict(X_test)

# Evaluate the classifier
print(classification_report(y_test, y_pred))
```

This code will output a classification report that includes metrics such as precision, recall, and F1 score for each sentiment category.

Image processing with Python

Image processing is a fascinating field that involves analyzing and manipulating digital images using mathematical algorithms. Python provides many powerful tools and libraries for working with images, such as OpenCV, Pillow, and Scikit-Image.

Loading and Displaying Images
The first step in image processing is to load an image into Python. This can be done using the Pillow library, which provides functions for loading, manipulating, and saving images.

Here is an example of how to load and display an image using Pillow:

```python
from PIL import Image

# Load the image
img = Image.open('example.jpg')

# Display the image
img.show()
```

This code will display the image in a new window.

Manipulating Images

Once an image has been loaded into Python, it can be manipulated using various image processing techniques. For example, images can be resized, cropped, rotated, and filtered.

Here is an example of how to resize an image using Pillow:

```python
from PIL import Image

# Load the image
img = Image.open('example.jpg')

# Resize the image
new_size = (640, 480)
resized_img = img.resize(new_size)

# Save the resized image
resized_img.save('resized.jpg')

# Display the resized image
resized_img.show()
```

This code will resize the image to a new size of 640x480 pixels, save the resized image to a new file, and display the resized image in a new window.

Detecting Objects in Images

Another common application of image processing is object detection. This involves identifying objects in an image and drawing bounding boxes around them. OpenCV is a popular library for object detection in images.

Here is an example of how to detect faces in an image using OpenCV:

```python
import cv2

# Load the image
img = cv2.imread('example.jpg')

# Convert the image to grayscale
gray_img = cv2.cvtColor(img, cv2.COLOR_BGR2GRAY)

# Load the face detector
face_cascade = cv2.CascadeClassifier('haarcascade_frontalface_default.xml')

# Detect faces in the image
faces = face_cascade.detectMultiScale(gray_img, scaleFactor=1.1, minNeighbors=5)

# Draw bounding boxes around the faces
for (x, y, w, h) in faces:
    cv2.rectangle(img, (x, y), (x+w, y+h), (0, 255, 0), 2)

# Display the image with bounding boxes
cv2.imshow('Image', img)
cv2.waitKey(0)
cv2.destroyAllWindows()
```

This code will detect faces in the image using a pre-trained Haar Cascade classifier, draw bounding boxes around the faces, and display the image with the bounding boxes in a new window.

Enhancing Images

Finally, images can be enhanced using various image processing techniques. For example, images can be sharpened, blurred, or filtered to reduce noise.

Here is an example of how to apply a median filter to an image using Scikit-Image:

```python
from skimage.filters import median

# Load the image
img = Image.open('example.jpg')

# Convert the image to a NumPy array
img_array = np.array(img)
```

```
# Apply a median filter to the image
filtered_img = median(img_array, selem=np.ones((3,3)))

# Convert the filtered image back to a Pillow image
filtered_img = Image.fromarray(filtered_img)

# Save the filtered image
filtered_img.save('filtered.jpg')

# Display the filtered image
filtered_img.show()
```

This code will apply a median filter to the image to reduce noise, save the filtered image to a new file, and display the filtered image in a new window.

Using OpenCV for image processing in Python

OpenCV is a popular library for image processing and computer vision. It provides many functions for working with images, such as loading, displaying, manipulating, and analyzing images. In this text, we will explore some of the capabilities of OpenCV for image processing in Python.

Loading and Displaying Images
The first step in using OpenCV for image processing is to load an image into Python. This can be done using the imread() function, which reads an image from a file and returns a NumPy array representing the image.

Here is an example of how to load and display an image using OpenCV:

```
import cv2

# Load the image
img = cv2.imread('example.jpg')

# Display the image
cv2.imshow('Image', img)
cv2.waitKey(0)
cv2.destroyAllWindows()
```

This code will display the image in a new window using the imshow() function. The waitKey() function waits for a key event to occur (such as a key press) before closing the window, and the destroyAllWindows() function closes all windows.

Manipulating Images

Once an image has been loaded into OpenCV, it can be manipulated using various image processing techniques. For example, images can be resized, cropped, rotated, and filtered.

Here is an example of how to resize an image using OpenCV:

```
import cv2

# Load the image
img = cv2.imread('example.jpg')

# Resize the image
new_size = (640, 480)
resized_img = cv2.resize(img, new_size)
```

```
# Display the resized image
cv2.imshow('Resized Image', resized_img)
cv2.waitKey(0)
cv2.destroyAllWindows()
```

This code will resize the image to a new size of 640x480 pixels using the resize() function and display the resized image in a new window.

Detecting Objects in Images
Another common application of image processing is object detection. This involves identifying objects in an image and drawing bounding boxes around them. OpenCV provides many functions for object detection in images, such as face detection and object recognition.

Here is an example of how to detect faces in an image using OpenCV:

```
import cv2

# Load the image
img = cv2.imread('example.jpg')

# Convert the image to grayscale
gray_img = cv2.cvtColor(img, cv2.COLOR_BGR2GRAY)

# Load the face detector
face_cascade = cv2.CascadeClassifier('haarcascade_frontalface_default.xml')

# Detect faces in the image
faces = face_cascade.detectMultiScale(gray_img, scaleFactor=1.1, minNeighbors=5)

# Draw bounding boxes around the faces
for (x, y, w, h) in faces:
    cv2.rectangle(img, (x, y), (x+w, y+h), (0, 255, 0), 2)

# Display the image with bounding boxes
cv2.imshow('Image', img)
cv2.waitKey(0)
cv2.destroyAllWindows()
```

This code will detect faces in the image using a pre-trained Haar Cascade classifier, draw bounding boxes around the faces using the rectangle() function, and display the image with the bounding boxes in a new window.

Enhancing Images

Finally, images can be enhanced using various image processing techniques. For example, images can be sharpened, blurred, or filtered to reduce noise.

Here is an example of how to apply a median filter to an image using OpenCV:

```python
import cv2
import numpy as np

# Load the image
img = cv2.imread('example.jpg')

# Apply a median filter to the image
filtered_img = cv2.medianBlur(img, 3)

# Display the

filtered image
cv2.imshow('Filtered Image', filtered_img)
cv2.waitKey(0)
cv2.destroyAllWindows()
```

This code will apply a median filter with a kernel size of 3x3 to the image using the `medianBlur()` function and display the filtered image in a new window.

In this text, we have explored some of the capabilities of OpenCV for image processing in Python. We have shown how to load and display images, manipulate images, detect objects in images, and enhance images using various image processing techniques. OpenCV is a powerful tool for working with images and can be used for a wide range of applications in computer vision and image processing.

Advanced data structures in Python

Python provides a variety of data structures that can be used for storing and manipulating data. In addition to the basic data structures such as lists and dictionaries, Python also provides advanced data structures that offer additional functionality and performance benefits. In this text, we will explore some of these advanced data structures and how they can be used in Python.

Tuples

Tuples are a simple data structure in Python that can be used for storing a sequence of values. Unlike lists, tuples are immutable, which means that their values cannot be changed once they are created. This makes tuples useful for representing data that should not be modified.

Here is an example of how to create and use tuples in Python:

```python
# Create a tuple
t = (1, 2, 3)

# Access tuple elements
print(t[0]) # Output: 1

# Iterate over tuple
for x in t:
    print(x)

# Output:
# 1
# 2
# 3
```

Sets

Sets are another advanced data structure in Python that can be used for storing collections of unique elements. Unlike lists and tuples, sets are unordered, which means that their elements do not have a specific order.

Here is an example of how to create and use sets in Python:

```python
# Create a set
s = {1, 2, 3}

# Add an element to the set
s.add(4)

# Remove an element from the set
```

```
s.remove(2)

# Check if an element is in the set
if 3 in s:
    print("3 is in the set")

# Output: 3 is in the set
```

Dictionaries

Dictionaries are a powerful data structure in Python that can be used for storing key-value pairs. Dictionaries allow fast lookup of values based on their keys, making them useful for many applications.

Here is an example of how to create and use dictionaries in Python:

```
# Create a dictionary
d = {'apple': 1, 'banana': 2, 'orange': 3}

# Access a value by key
print(d['banana']) # Output: 2

# Iterate over dictionary keys
for k in d:
    print(k)

# Output:
# apple
# banana
# orange
```

Named Tuples

Named tuples are a type of tuple in Python that allow the elements to be accessed by name instead of index. Named tuples can be useful for making code more readable and self-documenting.

Here is an example of how to create and use named tuples in Python:

```
from collections import namedtuple

# Create a named tuple
Person = namedtuple('Person', ['name', 'age'])

# Create an instance of the named tuple
p = Person('Alice', 30)
```

```
# Access the elements by name
print(p.name) # Output: Alice
print(p.age) # Output: 30
```

Deque

Deque, short for "double-ended queue", is a data structure in Python that can be used for efficiently adding and removing elements from both ends of the queue. Deques allow fast insertion and removal of elements at both ends, making them useful for implementing algorithms such as breadth-first search.

Here is an example of how to create and use deques in Python:

```
from collections import deque

# Create a deque
d = deque([1, 2, 3])

# Append an element to the right side
d.append(4)

# Append an element to the left side
d.appendleft(0)

# Pop an element from the right side
d.pop()

# Pop an element from the left side
d.popleft()

# Output: deque([0, 1, 2, 3])
```

In this text, we have explored some of the advanced data structures available in Python. Tuples, sets, dictionaries, named tuples, and deques offer additional functionality and performance benefits over the basic data structures provided by Python. Tuples are useful for representing immutable data, sets for storing collections of unique elements, dictionaries for storing key-value pairs, named tuples for making code more readable, and deques for efficiently adding and removing elements from both ends of a queue. By using these advanced data structures, you can write more efficient and readable code in Python.

Working with JSON data in Python

JSON (JavaScript Object Notation) is a popular data format for storing and exchanging data between different applications. Python provides built-in support for working with JSON data using the json module. In this text, we will explore how to work with JSON data in Python.

JSON Basics

JSON is a lightweight format for storing and exchanging data that is easy for humans to read and write and easy for machines to parse and generate. JSON data is represented as a collection of key-value pairs, where the keys are strings and the values can be strings, numbers, arrays, or other JSON objects. Here is an example of JSON data:

```
{
  "name": "John",
  "age": 30,
  "city": "New York",
  "hobbies": ["reading", "running", "traveling"],
  "job": {
    "title": "software engineer",
    "company": "Acme Inc."
  }
}
```

Loading JSON Data

To load JSON data into a Python program, we can use the json.loads() function, which takes a JSON string as input and returns a Python object that represents the JSON data. Here is an example:

```python
import json

# JSON string
json_string = '{"name": "John", "age": 30, "city": "New York"}'

# Load JSON data
data = json.loads(json_string)

# Access data
print(data['name']) # Output: John
print(data['age']) # Output: 30
```

Dumping JSON Data

To convert a Python object to JSON data, we can use the json.dumps() function, which takes a Python object as input and returns a JSON string that represents the object. Here is an example:

```python
import json

# Python object
data = {
  "name": "John",
  "age": 30,
  "city": "New York",
  "hobbies": ["reading", "running", "traveling"],
  "job": {
    "title": "software engineer",
    "company": "Acme Inc."
  }
}

# Convert to JSON data
json_data = json.dumps(data)

# Output JSON data
print(json_data)
```

Working with JSON Files

To load JSON data from a file, we can use the json.load() function, which takes a file object as input and returns a Python object that represents the JSON data. Here is an example:

```python
import json

# Open JSON file
with open('data.json') as f:
  # Load JSON data
  data = json.load(f)

# Access data
print(data['name']) # Output: John
print(data['age']) # Output: 30
```

To save Python data to a JSON file, we can use the json.dump() function, which takes a Python object and a file object as inputs and writes the JSON data to the file. Here is an example:

```python
import json

# Python object
data = {
  "name": "John",
  "age": 30,
  "city": "New York",
  "hobbies": ["reading", "running", "traveling"],
  "job": {
    "title": "software engineer",
    "company": "Acme Inc."
  }
}

# Save to JSON file
with open('data.json', 'w') as f:
  # Write JSON data
  json.dump(data, f)
```

Working with XML data in Python

XML (Extensible Markup Language) is a popular data format for storing and exchanging data between different applications. Python provides built-in support for working with XML data using the xml module. In this text, we will explore how to work with XML data in Python.

XML Basics
XML is a markup language that uses tags to define elements and attributes to provide additional information about those elements. XML data is represented as a hierarchical tree structure, where each element has a parent and zero or more child elements. Here is an example of XML data:

```
<people>
  <person id="1">
    <name>John</name>
    <age>30</age>
    <city>New York</city>
  </person>
  <person id="2">
    <name>Jane</name>
    <age>25</age>
    <city>Los Angeles</city>
  </person>
</people>
```

Loading XML Data

To load XML data into a Python program, we can use the xml.etree.ElementTree module, which provides a simple way to parse XML data into an ElementTree object. Here is an example:

```
import xml.etree.ElementTree as ET

# XML data
xml_data = '''
<people>
  <person id="1">
    <name>John</name>
    <age>30</age>
    <city>New York</city>
  </person>
  <person id="2">
    <name>Jane</name>
    <age>25</age>
    <city>Los Angeles</city>
  </person>
</people>
```

```
# Parse XML data
tree = ET.ElementTree(ET.fromstring(xml_data))

# Get root element
root = tree.getroot()

# Access data
for person in root.findall('person'):
    print(person.find('name').text) # Output: John, Jane
    print(person.find('age').text) # Output: 30, 25
```

Dumping XML Data

To convert an ElementTree object to XML data, we can use the ET.tostring() function, which takes an Element object as input and returns an XML string that represents the object. Here is an example:

```
import xml.etree.ElementTree as ET

# Create ElementTree object
root = ET.Element('people')

# Add elements
person1 = ET.SubElement(root, 'person', {'id': '1'})
name1 = ET.SubElement(person1, 'name')
name1.text = 'John'
age1 = ET.SubElement(person1, 'age')
age1.text = '30'
city1 = ET.SubElement(person1, 'city')
city1.text = 'New York'

person2 = ET.SubElement(root, 'person', {'id': '2'})
name2 = ET.SubElement(person2, 'name')
name2.text = 'Jane'
age2 = ET.SubElement(person2, 'age')
age2.text = '25'
city2 = ET.SubElement(person2, 'city')
city2.text = 'Los Angeles'

# Convert to XML data
xml_data = ET.tostring(root)

# Output XML data
print(xml_data)
```

Working with XML Files

To load XML data from a file, we can use the ET.parse() function, which takes a file object as input and returns an ElementTree object that represents the XML data. Here is an example:

```python
import xml.etree.ElementTree as ET

# Parse XML file
tree = ET.parse('data.xml')

# Get root element
root = tree.getroot()

# Access data
for person in root.findall('person'):
    print(person.find('name').text) # Output: John, Jane
```

Working with XML Attributes
In XML, attributes provide additional information about an element. To access attributes in Python, we can use the attrib attribute of an Element object. Here is an example:

```python
import xml.etree.ElementTree as ET

# XML data with attributes
xml_data = '''
<people>
  <person id="1">
    <name>John</name>
    <age>30</age>
    <city>New York</city>
  </person>
  <person id="2">
    <name>Jane</name>
    <age>25</age>
    <city>Los Angeles</city>
  </person>
</people>
'''

# Parse XML data
tree = ET.ElementTree(ET.fromstring(xml_data))

# Get root element
root = tree.getroot()

# Access attributes
for person in root.findall('person'):
    print(person.attrib['id']) # Output: 1, 2
```

Working with Namespaces

XML namespaces are used to avoid name collisions in XML documents. To work with namespaces in Python, we can use the namespaces parameter of the ET.Element() function to specify the namespace URI and prefix for an element. Here is an example:

```python
import xml.etree.ElementTree as ET

# XML data with namespaces
xml_data = '''
<ns:people xmlns:ns="http://example.com/ns">
  <ns:person id="1">
    <ns:name>John</ns:name>
    <ns:age>30</ns:age>
    <ns:city>New York</ns:city>
  </ns:person>
  <ns:person id="2">
    <ns:name>Jane</ns:name>
    <ns:age>25</ns:age>
    <ns:city>Los Angeles</ns:city>
  </ns:person>
</ns:people>
'''

# Parse XML data
tree = ET.ElementTree(ET.fromstring(xml_data))

# Get root element
root = tree.getroot()

# Access data using namespace prefix
for person in root.findall('ns:person', {'ns': 'http://example.com/ns'}):
    print(person.find('ns:name', {'ns': 'http://example.com/ns'}).text) # Output: John, Jane
    print(person.find('ns:age', {'ns': 'http://example.com/ns'}).text) # Output: 30, 25
```

In this text, we have explored how to work with XML data in Python using the xml.etree.ElementTree module. We have seen how to load XML data into a Python program, how to access and modify XML elements and attributes, how to convert ElementTree objects to XML data, and how to work with XML namespaces. By using these techniques, you can easily manipulate XML data in your Python applications.

Manipulating and analyzing CSV files with Python

CSV (Comma Separated Values) files are a popular way to store and exchange data in a tabular format. In this text, we will explore how to manipulate and analyze CSV files using Python.

Reading CSV Files with Python
Python has built-in support for reading CSV files using the csv module. Here is an example of how to read a CSV file:

```python
import csv

# Open CSV file
with open('data.csv', 'r') as csvfile:
    # Create reader object
    reader = csv.reader(csvfile)

    # Iterate over rows
    for row in reader:
        print(row)
```

In this example, we first open the CSV file using the open() function and create a csv.reader object by passing the file object to the csv.reader() function. We then iterate over the rows of the CSV file using a for loop and print each row to the console.

Writing CSV Files with Python

Python also has built-in support for writing CSV files using the csv module. Here is an example of how to write a CSV file:

```python
import csv

# Open CSV file for writing
with open('output.csv', 'w', newline='') as csvfile:
    # Create writer object
    writer = csv.writer(csvfile)

    # Write header row
    writer.writerow(['Name', 'Age', 'City'])

    # Write data rows
    writer.writerow(['John', '30', 'New York'])
    writer.writerow(['Jane', '25', 'Los Angeles'])
```

In this example, we first open the CSV file for writing using the open() function and create a csv.writer object by passing the file object to the csv.writer() function. We then write the header row and data rows to the CSV file using the writerow() method of the writer object.

Manipulating CSV Data with Python

Python provides several ways to manipulate CSV data. For example, we can use the csv.DictReader class to read CSV data into a dictionary, where each row is represented by a dictionary with keys corresponding to the column names. Here is an example:

```python
import csv

# Open CSV file
with open('data.csv', 'r') as csvfile:
    # Create reader object
    reader = csv.DictReader(csvfile)

    # Iterate over rows
    for row in reader:
        print(row['Name'], row['Age'], row['City'])
```

In this example, we first open the CSV file using the open() function and create a csv.DictReader object by passing the file object to the csv.DictReader() function. We then iterate over the rows of the CSV file using a for loop and print the values of the 'Name', 'Age', and 'City' columns to the console.

Analyzing CSV Data with Python

Python also provides powerful libraries for analyzing CSV data, such as pandas. Here is an example of how to use pandas to read a CSV file, perform some analysis, and write the results to a new CSV file:

```python
import pandas as pd

# Read CSV file into DataFrame
df = pd.read_csv('data.csv')

# Group data by city and compute average age
result = df.groupby('City').agg({'Age': 'mean'})

# Write result to new CSV file
result.to_csv('output.csv')
```

In this example, we first use pandas to read the CSV file into a DataFrame object. We then use the groupby() method of the DataFrame object to group the data by city and compute the average age using the mean() method. Finally, we use the to_csv() method of the result object to write the results to a new CSV file.

Handling Large CSV Files with Python

Handling large CSV files can be challenging, as reading and writing large amounts of data can cause memory errors. To handle large CSV files in Python, we can use the csv module's reader and writer objects to process the data one row at a time. Here is an example:

```python
import csv

# Open input and output CSV files
with open('input.csv', 'r') as inputfile, open('output.csv', 'w', newline='') as outputfile:
    # Create reader and writer objects
    reader = csv.reader(inputfile)
    writer = csv.writer(outputfile)

    # Write header row to output file
    writer.writerow(['Name', 'Age', 'City'])

    # Iterate over rows of input file and write selected rows to output file
    for row in reader:
        if row[2] == 'New York':
            writer.writerow(row)
```

In this example, we first open the input and output CSV files using the open() function and create a csv.reader and csv.writer object by passing the file objects to the csv.reader() and csv.writer() functions. We then write the header row to the output file using the writerow() method of the writer object. Finally, we iterate over the rows of the input file using a for loop and write selected rows to the output file using the writerow() method of the writer object.

In this text, we have explored how to manipulate and analyze CSV files using Python. We have learned how to read and write CSV files, manipulate CSV data using the csv module's DictReader class, analyze CSV data using pandas, and handle large CSV files by processing the data one row at a time. With these techniques, you can effectively work with CSV files in your Python projects.

SQLite database programming in Python

Introduction to SQLite Database Programming in Python
SQLite is a popular open-source relational database management system that is lightweight, fast, and easy to use. SQLite is ideal for small to medium-sized databases and is widely used in mobile applications, web browsers, and embedded systems. Python provides a built-in sqlite3 module that allows us to interact with SQLite databases.

Connecting to a SQLite Database in Python
Before we can perform any operations on a SQLite database in Python, we need to establish a connection to the database. Here is an example:

```python
import sqlite3

# Connect to a SQLite database
conn = sqlite3.connect('example.db')

# Create a cursor object
cur = conn.cursor()
```

In this example, we first import the sqlite3 module and then use the connect() method of the module to establish a connection to a SQLite database named example.db. We then create a cursor object using the cursor() method of the connection object.

Creating Tables in a SQLite Database using Python

Once we have established a connection to a SQLite database, we can create tables in the database using the CREATE TABLE statement. Here is an example:

```python
# Create a table
cur.execute('''CREATE TABLE users
        (id INTEGER PRIMARY KEY, name TEXT, email TEXT, age INTEGER)''')
```

In this example, we use the execute() method of the cursor object to execute a CREATE TABLE statement that creates a table named users with four columns: id, name, email, and age. The id column is defined as an integer primary key.

Inserting Data into a SQLite Database using Python

Once we have created a table in a SQLite database, we can insert data into the table using the INSERT INTO statement. Here is an example:

```python
# Insert data into the table
cur.execute("INSERT INTO users (name, email, age) VALUES (?, ?, ?)", ('John', 'john@example.com', 30))
```

In this example, we use the execute() method of the cursor object to execute an INSERT INTO statement that inserts a row into the users table with the values John, john@example.com, and 30 for the name, email, and age columns, respectively. We use parameterized queries to prevent SQL injection attacks.

Selecting Data from a SQLite Database using Python

Once we have inserted data into a table in a SQLite database, we can select data from the table using the SELECT statement. Here is an example:

```
# Select data from the table
cur.execute("SELECT * FROM users")

# Fetch all rows
rows = cur.fetchall()

# Print the rows
for row in rows:
    print(row)
```

In this example, we use the execute() method of the cursor object to execute a SELECT statement that selects all rows from the users table. We then use the fetchall() method of the cursor object to fetch all the rows and store them in the rows variable. Finally, we use a for loop to print the rows.

Updating Data in a SQLite Database using Python

Once we have selected data from a table in a SQLite database, we can update data in the table using the UPDATE statement. Here is an example:

```
# Update data in the table
cur.execute("UPDATE users SET age = ? WHERE name = ?", (40, 'John'))
```

In this example, we use the execute() method of the cursor object to execute an UPDATE statement that updates the age column of the row in the users table with the name `John.

Deleting Data from a SQLite Database using Python

Once we have selected data from a table in a SQLite database, we can delete data from the table using the DELETE statement. Here is an example:

```
# Delete data from the table
cur.execute("DELETE FROM users WHERE name = ?", ('John',))
```

In this example, we use the execute() method of the cursor object to execute a DELETE statement that deletes the row with the name John from the users table. We use a parameterized query to prevent SQL injection attacks.

Committing Changes to a SQLite Database using Python

Whenever we make changes to a SQLite database in Python, such as inserting data, updating data, or deleting data, we need to commit the changes using the commit() method of the connection object. Here is an example:

```
# Commit the changes
conn.commit()
```

In this example, we use the commit() method of the connection object to commit the changes made to the database.

Closing a SQLite Database Connection in Python

Whenever we finish working with a SQLite database in Python, we should close the connection to the database using the close() method of the connection object. Here is an example:

```
# Close the connection
conn.close()
```

In this example, we use the close() method of the connection object to close the connection to the database.

In this tutorial, we have learned how to work with SQLite databases in Python using the built-in sqlite3 module. We have learned how to establish a connection to a database, create tables, insert data, select data, update data, delete data, commit changes, and close the connection. With these skills, we can manipulate data in SQLite databases using Python.

MySQL database programming in Python

Connecting to a MySQL Database in Python
To connect to a MySQL database in Python, we need to install the mysql-connector-python module. Once we have installed the module, we can connect to the database using the connect() function provided by the module. Here is an example:

```python
import mysql.connector

# Connect to the database
conn = mysql.connector.connect(
    host="localhost",
    user="username",
    password="password",
    database="mydatabase"
)
```

In this example, we use the connect() function of the mysql.connector module to connect to a MySQL database running on localhost. We provide the username, password, and database name as parameters to the function.

Creating Tables in a MySQL Database using Python
Once we have connected to a MySQL database in Python, we can create tables using SQL CREATE TABLE statements. Here is an example:

```python
# Create a table
cur = conn.cursor()
cur.execute("CREATE TABLE users (id INT AUTO_INCREMENT PRIMARY KEY, name VARCHAR(255), email VARCHAR(255))")
```

In this example, we use the execute() method of the cursor object to execute a SQL CREATE TABLE statement that creates a table named users with three columns: id, name, and email. The id column is an auto-incrementing primary key.

Inserting Data into a MySQL Database using Python

Once we have created a table in a MySQL database using Python, we can insert data into the table using SQL INSERT INTO statements. Here is an example:

```python
# Insert data into the table
cur.execute("INSERT INTO users (name, email) VALUES (%s, %s)", ('John', 'john@example.com'))
```

In this example, we use the execute() method of the cursor object to execute a SQL INSERT INTO statement that inserts a row with the name John and the email john@example.com into the users table. We use a parameterized query to prevent SQL injection attacks.

Selecting Data from a MySQL Database using Python

Once we have inserted data into a table in a MySQL database using Python, we can select data from the table using SQL SELECT statements. Here is an example:

```
# Select data from the table
cur.execute("SELECT * FROM users")
result = cur.fetchall()
for row in result:
    print(row)
```

In this example, we use the execute() method of the cursor object to execute a SQL SELECT statement that selects all columns from the users table. We use the fetchall() method of the cursor object to fetch all rows returned by the query, and we loop through the rows and print them to the console.

Updating Data in a MySQL Database using Python
Once we have selected data from a table in a MySQL database using Python, we can update data in the table using SQL UPDATE statements. Here is an example:

```
# Update data in the table
cur.execute("UPDATE users SET email = %s WHERE name = %s", ('jane@example.com', 'Jane'))
```

In this example, we use the execute() method of the cursor object to execute a SQL UPDATE statement that updates the email column of the row with the name Jane in the users table.

Deleting Data from a MySQL Database using Python

Once we have selected data from a table in a MySQL database using Python, we can delete data from the table using SQL DELETE statements. Here is an example:

```
# Delete data from the table
delete_query = "DELETE FROM users WHERE name = %s"
cur.execute(delete_query, ('John',))
```

In this example, we first define the SQL DELETE statement as a string variable delete_query. The %s placeholder is used to represent the value that we want to delete, which in this case is 'John'. We then execute the SQL statement using the execute() method of the cursor object, passing the delete_query and a tuple containing the value to be deleted as arguments. This ensures that the value is properly escaped and prevents SQL injection attacks.

Closing the Connection to a MySQL Database in Python

Once we are finished working with a MySQL database in Python, we should close the connection to the database to free up resources. Here is an example:

```
# Close the connection to the database
conn.close()
```

In this example, we use the close() method of the connection object to close the connection to the MySQL database.

In this tutorial, we have seen how to connect to a MySQL database in Python using the mysql-connector-python module, how to create tables, insert data, select data, update data, and delete data in the database using SQL statements, and how to close the connection to the database. With this knowledge, you can start building applications that interact with MySQL databases in Python.

PostgreSQL database programming in Python

PostgreSQL database programming in Python is a popular choice for many developers. It offers a powerful and flexible database management system that can be easily integrated with Python code.

To get started with PostgreSQL in Python, you first need to install the psycopg2 module. This module provides a Python interface to the PostgreSQL database and allows you to interact with it from your Python code.

Once you have installed the psycopg2 module, you can connect to your PostgreSQL database using the following code:

```
import psycopg2

conn = psycopg2.connect(
    host="yourhost",
    database="yourdatabase",
    user="yourusername",
    password="yourpassword"
)
```

This code creates a connection object to your PostgreSQL database, which you can use to execute SQL queries and transactions.

To execute a SQL query, you can use the cursor method of your connection object. For example, the following code executes a simple SQL query to retrieve all rows from a table named users:

```
cursor = conn.cursor()
cursor.execute("SELECT * FROM users")
rows = cursor.fetchall()
```

This code creates a cursor object, executes the SQL query, and retrieves all the rows from the users table.

You can also execute more complex SQL queries using parameterized queries. Parameterized queries help protect against SQL injection attacks by allowing you to pass user input as parameters instead of directly inserting them into your SQL query. For example, the following code executes a parameterized SQL query to retrieve all rows from a table named users where the age column is greater than a user-specified value:

This code prompts the user to enter a value for the age parameter, and then executes the parameterized SQL query using the execute method of the cursor object.

In addition to executing SQL queries, you can also perform transactions using the commit and rollback methods of your connection object. For example, the following code performs a transaction to insert a new row into a table named users:

```
cursor = conn.cursor()
cursor.execute("INSERT INTO users (name, age) VALUES ('John', 30)")
conn.commit()
```

This code creates a cursor object, executes an SQL query to insert a new row into the users table, and then commits the transaction using the commit method of the connection object.

In conclusion, PostgreSQL database programming in Python offers a powerful and flexible way to manage your database. By using the psycopg2 module and the techniques described in this text, you can easily integrate your Python code with your PostgreSQL database and perform a wide range of SQL queries and transactions.

MongoDB programming in Python

MongoDB Programming in Python is a popular choice for developers who want a flexible and scalable NoSQL database. It offers many features that make it a great option for managing data-intensive applications, such as real-time analytics, IoT applications, and social media platforms. In this text, we'll explore some of the key features of MongoDB programming in Python, and how you can use it to build powerful and scalable applications.

Connecting to MongoDB in Python

To get started with MongoDB in Python, you first need to install the PyMongo module. This module provides a Python interface to the MongoDB database and allows you to interact with it from your Python code.

Once you have installed the PyMongo module, you can connect to your MongoDB database using the following code:

import pymongo

```
client = pymongo.MongoClient("mongodb://localhost:27017/")
db = client["mydatabase"]
```

MongoDB Programming in Python is a popular choice for developers who want a flexible and scalable NoSQL database. It offers many features that make it a great option for managing data-intensive applications, such as real-time analytics, IoT applications, and social media platforms. In this text, we'll explore some of the key features of MongoDB programming in Python, and how you can use it to build powerful and scalable applications.

Connecting to MongoDB in Python

To get started with MongoDB in Python, you first need to install the PyMongo module. This module provides a Python interface to the MongoDB database and allows you to interact with it from your Python code.

Once you have installed the PyMongo module, you can connect to your MongoDB database using the following code:

```
java
Copy code
import pymongo
```

```
client = pymongo.MongoClient("mongodb://localhost:27017/")
db = client["mydatabase"]
```

This code creates a client object to your MongoDB database, which you can use to execute queries and transactions.

Inserting Data into MongoDB

To insert data into MongoDB using Python, you can use the insert_one() or insert_many() methods of your database object. For example, the following code inserts a new document into a collection named users:

```
user = {"name": "John", "age": 30}
users_collection = db["users"]
users_collection.insert_one(user)
```

This code creates a new document object, inserts it into the users collection using the insert_one() method, and then saves it to the database.

Querying Data in MongoDB

To query data in MongoDB using Python, you can use the find() method of your collection object. For example, the following code retrieves all documents from the users collection:

```
users_collection = db["users"]
users = users_collection.find()
for user in users:
    print(user)
```

This code retrieves all documents from the users collection using the find() method, and then iterates over them using a for loop.

Updating Data in MongoDB

To update data in MongoDB using Python, you can use the update_one() or update_many() methods of your collection object. For example, the following code updates a document in the users collection:

```
users_collection = db["users"]
query = {"name": "John"}
new_values = {"$set": {"age": 40}}
users_collection.update_one(query, new_values)
```

This code creates a query object to find the document with the name "John", updates its age to 40 using the $set operator, and then updates the document in the users collection using the update_one() method.

Deleting Data in MongoDB

To delete data in MongoDB using Python, you can use the delete_one() or delete_many() methods of your collection object. For example, the following code deletes a document from the users collection:

```
users_collection = db["users"]
query = {"name": "John"}
users_collection.delete_one(query)
```

This code creates a query object to find the document with the name "John", and then deletes it from the users collection using the delete_one() method.

MongoDB programming in Python offers a flexible and scalable way to manage your data. By using the PyMongo module and the techniques described in this text, you can easily integrate your Python code with your MongoDB database and perform a wide range of queries and transactions. With its powerful features and flexible schema design, MongoDB is a great choice for building modern and data-intensive applications.

PySpark programming for big data analysis

PySpark programming is a powerful tool for big data analysis. With its ability to handle large-scale data processing and its integration with Python, it has become a popular choice for data scientists and developers. In this text, we'll explore some of the key features of PySpark programming and how you can use it to perform big data analysis.

Setting up PySpark in Python

To get started with PySpark programming in Python, you first need to install the PySpark module. This module provides a Python interface to the Apache Spark platform, which is used for large-scale data processing.

Once you have installed the PySpark module, you can create a SparkSession object to interact with the Spark platform. For example, the following code creates a SparkSession object and sets the application name:

```
from pyspark.sql import SparkSession
```

```
spark = SparkSession.builder.appName("myApp").getOrCreate()
```

This code creates a SparkSession object named spark and sets the application name to "myApp".

Loading Data into PySpark

To load data into PySpark, you can use the read method of your SparkSession object. For example, the following code loads a CSV file into a PySpark DataFrame:

```
data = spark.read.csv("mydata.csv", header=True, inferSchema=True)
```

This code reads a CSV file named "mydata.csv" and creates a PySpark DataFrame object named data. The header and inferSchema parameters are used to specify whether the file has a header row and to automatically infer the data types of the columns.

Transforming Data in PySpark

Once you have loaded data into PySpark, you can use its powerful transformation capabilities to manipulate and analyze the data. PySpark provides many built-in functions and operations for data transformation, such as filtering, grouping, and aggregation.

For example, the following code groups the data by a column named "category" and calculates the average value of another column named "value":

grouped_data = data.groupBy("category").avg("value")

This code groups the data in the data DataFrame by the "category" column using the groupBy() method, and then calculates the average value of the "value" column using the avg() method.

Running Machine Learning Algorithms in PySpark

PySpark also provides a powerful machine learning library called MLlib. This library provides a wide range of machine learning algorithms, such as regression, classification, and clustering.

For example, the following code trains a linear regression model on some data and makes predictions on a test dataset:

```
from pyspark.ml.regression import LinearRegression
from pyspark.ml.evaluation import RegressionEvaluator

# Split the data into training and test sets
(training_data, test_data) = data.randomSplit([0.7, 0.3])

# Train the model
lr = LinearRegression(featuresCol="features", labelCol="label")
model = lr.fit(training_data)

# Make predictions on the test dataset
predictions = model.transform(test_data)

# Evaluate the model
evaluator        =        RegressionEvaluator(predictionCol="prediction",        labelCol="label",
metricName="rmse")
rmse = evaluator.evaluate(predictions)
```

This code splits the data into training and test datasets using the randomSplit() method, trains a linear regression model on the training data using the LinearRegression() class, and then makes predictions on the test data using the transform() method. Finally, it evaluates the model using the RegressionEvaluator() class and calculates the root mean squared error (RMSE) of the predictions.

PySpark programming provides a powerful and flexible tool for big data analysis. By using its powerful transformation capabilities and built-in machine learning algorithms, you can easily analyze and manipulate large

Data preprocessing in Python for machine learning

Data preprocessing is an important step in preparing data for machine learning models. In this text, we'll explore some common data preprocessing techniques in Python and how you can use them to prepare your data for machine learning.

Handling Missing Data

Missing data is a common issue in real-world datasets. It can occur due to various reasons such as errors in data collection or processing, or simply because the data is not available.

To handle missing data, you can use the fillna() method of a Pandas DataFrame object to fill the missing values with a specified value or a statistical measure such as the mean or median. For example, the following code replaces missing values in a DataFrame with the mean of each column:

```
import pandas as pd

# Load the data
data = pd.read_csv("mydata.csv")

# Replace missing values with the mean of each column
data = data.fillna(data.mean())
```

This code loads a CSV file named "mydata.csv" into a Pandas DataFrame object named data, and then fills any missing values with the mean of each column using the fillna() method.

Handling Categorical Data

Categorical data is data that represents categories or labels, such as gender, color, or country. Machine learning models typically require numerical data, so you need to convert categorical data into numerical data.

To convert categorical data, you can use one-hot encoding or label encoding. One-hot encoding creates a binary vector for each category, while label encoding assigns a unique integer to each category.

For example, the following code uses label encoding to convert a categorical column named "gender" into numerical data:

```
from sklearn.preprocessing import LabelEncoder
```

```
# Load the data
data = pd.read_csv("mydata.csv")

# Encode the gender column
encoder = LabelEncoder()
data["gender"] = encoder.fit_transform(data["gender"])
```

This code loads a CSV file named "mydata.csv" into a Pandas DataFrame object named data, and then uses the LabelEncoder() class from the scikit-learn library to encode the "gender" column into numerical data.

Scaling and Normalizing Data

Machine learning models can be sensitive to the scale of the data. For example, if one feature has a much larger range of values than another feature, it can dominate the model's predictions.

To address this issue, you can scale or normalize the data. Scaling involves transforming the data so that it has a specific range, such as between 0 and 1. Normalizing involves transforming the data so that it has a specific distribution, such as a standard normal distribution.

For example, the following code uses the MinMaxScaler() class from the scikit-learn library to scale a DataFrame:

```
from sklearn.preprocessing import MinMaxScaler

# Load the data
data = pd.read_csv("mydata.csv")

# Scale the data
scaler = MinMaxScaler()
data_scaled = scaler.fit_transform(data)
```

This code loads a CSV file named "mydata.csv" into a Pandas DataFrame object named data, and then scales the data using the MinMaxScaler() class from the scikit-learn library.

Data preprocessing is an essential step in preparing data for machine learning models. By handling missing data, converting categorical data, and scaling or normalizing the data, you can improve the accuracy and reliability of your machine learning models. Using the techniques discussed in this text, you can easily prepare your data for machine learning in Python.

Feature engineering for machine learning in Python

Feature engineering is an important step in the process of building machine learning models. It involves selecting and transforming the variables, or features, that will be used as inputs to the model. In this text, we will explore some common feature engineering techniques and demonstrate how to implement them in Python.

Data Cleaning and Preprocessing

Before we can start engineering features, we need to ensure that the data is clean and well-prepared. This includes handling missing values, dealing with outliers, and encoding categorical variables. Here is an example of how to handle missing values using Pandas:

```python
import pandas as pd

# Load data
df = pd.read_csv('data.csv')

# Identify missing values
missing = df.isnull().sum()

# Replace missing values with the mean
df.fillna(df.mean(), inplace=True)
```

Feature Scaling

Machine learning algorithms often require that features be scaled to a similar range. This is because some algorithms are sensitive to the magnitude of the features, and scaling can help prevent one feature from dominating the others. Here is an example of how to scale features using Scikit-learn:

```python
from sklearn.preprocessing import StandardScaler

# Load data
X = pd.read_csv('data.csv').drop('target', axis=1)
y = df['target']

# Initialize scaler
scaler = StandardScaler()

# Fit scaler to the data
scaler.fit(X)

# Transform the data
X_scaled = scaler.transform(X)
```

Feature Selection

Not all features are equally important for predicting the target variable. Feature selection techniques can be used to identify the most relevant features and remove the rest. Here is an example of how to perform feature selection using Scikit-learn:

```python
from sklearn.feature_selection import SelectKBest, f_regression

# Load data
X = pd.read_csv('data.csv').drop('target', axis=1)
y = df['target']

# Initialize feature selector
selector = SelectKBest(f_regression, k=3)

# Fit selector to the data
selector.fit(X, y)

# Transform the data
X_selected = selector.transform(X)
```

Feature Encoding

Categorical variables need to be encoded in a numeric format before they can be used as inputs to machine learning algorithms. There are several methods for encoding categorical variables, including one-hot encoding and label encoding. Here is an example of how to perform one-hot encoding using Pandas:

```python
# Load data
df = pd.read_csv('data.csv')

# One-hot encode categorical variables
df_encoded = pd.get_dummies(df, columns=['category'])
```

In conclusion, feature engineering is a critical step in the process of building machine learning models. It involves selecting and transforming the variables that will be used as inputs to the model. In this text, we demonstrated some common feature engineering techniques and provided examples of how to implement them in Python using libraries such as Pandas and Scikit-learn.

Model selection and evaluation in machine learning with Python

Model selection and evaluation are essential steps in the process of building machine learning models. The goal of model selection is to choose the best algorithm and hyperparameters for a particular task, while the goal of model evaluation is to assess the performance of the chosen model. In this text, we will explore some common techniques for model selection and evaluation and demonstrate how to implement them in Python.

Train-test split

The train-test split is a simple technique for evaluating the performance of a model. It involves splitting the data into two sets: a training set and a testing set. The training set is used to train the model, while the testing set is used to evaluate its performance. Here is an example of how to perform a train-test split using Scikit-learn:

```
from sklearn.model_selection import train_test_split

# Load data
X = pd.read_csv('data.csv').drop('target', axis=1)
y = df['target']

# Split the data into training and testing sets
X_train, X_test, y_train, y_test = train_test_split(X, y, test_size=0.2, random_state=42)
```

Cross-validation

Cross-validation is a more robust technique for model evaluation than the train-test split. It involves dividing the data into k folds and training the model on k-1 folds while using the remaining fold for validation. This process is repeated k times, with each fold being used once for validation. Here is an example of how to perform cross-validation using Scikit-learn:

```
from sklearn.model_selection import cross_val_score
from sklearn.linear_model import LogisticRegression

# Load data
X = pd.read_csv('data.csv').drop('target', axis=1)
y = df['target']

# Initialize model
model = LogisticRegression()

# Perform cross-validation
scores = cross_val_score(model, X, y, cv=5)
```

Hyperparameter tuning

Most machine learning algorithms have hyperparameters that need to be tuned to achieve optimal performance. Hyperparameter tuning involves searching for the best combination of hyperparameters for a particular algorithm. One common technique for hyperparameter tuning is grid search, which involves searching over a predefined set of hyperparameters. Here is an example of how to perform grid search using Scikit-learn:

```python
from sklearn.model_selection import GridSearchCV
from sklearn.svm import SVC

    # Load data
    X = pd.read_csv('data.csv').drop('target', axis=1)
    y = df['target']

    # Define hyperparameters to search over
    params = {
        'C': [0.1, 1, 10],
        'kernel': ['linear', 'rbf', 'poly']
    }

    # Initialize model
    model = SVC()

    # Perform grid search
    grid_search = GridSearchCV(model, params, cv=5)
    grid_search.fit(X, y)

    # Print the best hyperparameters
    print(grid_search.best_params_)
```

In conclusion, model selection and evaluation are critical steps in the process of building machine learning models. In this text, we demonstrated some common techniques for model selection and evaluation, including the train-test split, cross-validation, and hyperparameter tuning. We also provided examples of how to implement these techniques in Python using libraries such as Scikit-learn.

Time series analysis with Python

Time series analysis is a powerful tool for analyzing data that changes over time. It is used in a variety of fields, including finance, economics, and weather forecasting. In this text, we will explore some common techniques for time series analysis and demonstrate how to implement them in Python.

Data preparation

The first step in time series analysis is to prepare the data. This involves cleaning and transforming the data to make it suitable for analysis. One common technique for data preparation is to resample the data to a lower frequency to reduce noise and make the patterns in the data more visible. Here is an example of how to prepare time series data using Pandas:

```python
import pandas as pd

# Load data
data = pd.read_csv('data.csv', index_col='date', parse_dates=True)

# Resample data to weekly frequency
data_weekly = data.resample('W').mean()
```

Visualization

Visualizing time series data is an essential step in understanding the patterns and trends in the data. One common visualization technique is to plot the data over time. Here is an example of how to visualize time series data using Matplotlib:

```python
import matplotlib.pyplot as plt

# Plot time series data
plt.plot(data_weekly)
plt.show()
```

Time series decomposition

Time series decomposition is a technique for separating a time series into its underlying components, including the trend, seasonality, and noise. Decomposing a time series can help identify patterns in the data and make it easier to forecast future values. Here is an example of how to decompose a time series using statsmodels:

```python
from statsmodels.tsa.seasonal import seasonal_decompose

# Decompose time series
decomposition = seasonal_decompose(data_weekly)
```

211

```
# Plot decomposition
trend = decomposition.trend
seasonal = decomposition.seasonal
residual = decomposition.resid

plt.subplot(411)
plt.plot(data_weekly, label='Original')
plt.legend(loc='best')
plt.subplot(412)
plt.plot(trend, label='Trend')
plt.legend(loc='best')
plt.subplot(413)
plt.plot(seasonal,label='Seasonality')
plt.legend(loc='best')
plt.subplot(414)
plt.plot(residual, label='Residuals')
plt.legend(loc='best')
plt.tight_layout()
plt.show()
```

Forecasting

Forecasting is the process of predicting future values of a time series based on its past values. There are many techniques for time series forecasting, including ARIMA, exponential smoothing, and Prophet. Here is an example of how to forecast a time series using Prophet:

```
from fbprophet import Prophet

# Prepare data for Prophet
data_prophet = pd.DataFrame({'ds': data_weekly.index, 'y': data_weekly.values})

# Initialize Prophet model
model = Prophet()

# Fit model to data
model.fit(data_prophet)

# Make predictions
future = model.make_future_dataframe(periods=365)
forecast = model.predict(future)

# Plot forecast
model.plot(forecast)
plt.show()
```

In conclusion, time series analysis is a powerful tool for analyzing data that changes over time. In this text, we explored some common techniques for time series analysis, including data preparation, visualization, time series decomposition, and forecasting.

We also provided examples of how to implement these techniques in Python using libraries such as Pandas, Matplotlib, statsmodels, and Prophet.

Signal processing with Python

Introduction to Signal Processing
Signal processing is a fundamental field in computer science and engineering that deals with the analysis, manipulation, and interpretation of signals. Signals can represent various types of data, such as audio, images, or sensor measurements. Python, with its rich set of libraries and tools, provides a powerful environment for signal processing tasks. In this tutorial, we will explore some key concepts and demonstrate how to perform signal processing tasks using Python.

Installing the Required Libraries

Before we dive into signal processing with Python, let's make sure we have the necessary libraries installed. We will primarily use the following libraries:

NumPy: A fundamental library for numerical computing in Python, which provides powerful array operations and linear algebra functions.

pip install numpy

SciPy: A library built on top of NumPy, providing a wide range of scientific computing functions, including signal processing routines.

pip install scipy

Matplotlib: A plotting library that enables us to visualize our signals and analysis results.

pip install matplotlib

PyWavelets: A library for wavelet analysis, which is a powerful tool for time-frequency analysis of signals.

pip install PyWavelets

Once we have installed these libraries, we can begin with our signal processing tasks.

Loading and Visualizing Signals
Before processing signals, we need to load and visualize them. Python provides various ways to load signals, depending on the signal type and format. Let's consider an example where we have an audio signal in WAV format. We can use the SciPy library to load the signal as follows:

```
from scipy.io import wavfile

# Load the audio signal
sample_rate, signal = wavfile.read('audio.wav')
```

After loading the signal, we can use Matplotlib to visualize it:

```
import matplotlib.pyplot as plt

# Plot the signal
plt.plot(signal)
plt.xlabel('Time')
plt.ylabel('Amplitude')
plt.show()
```

Signal Filtering

Filtering is a common signal processing operation that involves removing or attenuating certain frequencies from a signal. It can be useful for noise removal, smoothing, or isolating specific frequency components. In Python, we can apply various filters using the SciPy library. Let's consider an example where we apply a low-pass filter to an audio signal:

```
from scipy import signal

# Design the filter
cutoff_freq = 2000  # Cutoff frequency in Hz
nyquist_freq = 0.5 * sample_rate
normal_cutoff = cutoff_freq / nyquist_freq
b, a = signal.butter(4, normal_cutoff, btype='low', analog=False, output='ba')

# Apply the filter to the signal
filtered_signal = signal.lfilter(b, a, signal)

# Plot the original and filtered signals
plt.subplot(2, 1, 1)
plt.plot(signal)
plt.xlabel('Time')
plt.ylabel('Amplitude')
plt.title('Original Signal')

plt.subplot(2, 1, 2)
plt.plot(filtered_signal)
plt.xlabel('Time')
plt.ylabel('Amplitude')
plt.title('Filtered Signal')

plt.tight_layout()
plt.show()
```

Signal Transformation: Fourier Analysis

Fourier analysis is a technique used to transform a signal from the time domain to the frequency domain. It allows us to examine the frequency content of a signal and identify dominant frequency components. Python provides various functions for performing Fourier analysis, including the Fast Fourier Transform (FFT) algorithm in the NumPy library. Let's consider an example where we compute the magnitude spectrum of an audio signal:

```python
# Compute the magnitude spectrum using FFT
freq_bins = np.fft.fftfreq(len(signal),

signal.shape[0])
magnitude_spectrum = np.abs(np.fft.fft(signal))

Plot the magnitude spectrum
plt.plot(freq_bins, magnitude_spectrum)
plt.xlabel('Frequency')
plt.ylabel('Magnitude')
plt.title('Magnitude Spectrum')
plt.show()
```

Signal Compression: Wavelet Transform

Wavelet transform is a powerful technique for signal compression and time-frequency analysis. It allows us to represent a signal in terms of wavelet coefficients, which capture both time and frequency information. Python provides the PyWavelets library, which offers a wide range of wavelet analysis functions. Let's consider an example where we perform wavelet compression on an image:

```python
import pywt

# Perform wavelet decomposition
coeffs = pywt.wavedec2(image, 'haar', level=2)

# Set a threshold for compression
threshold = 0.1 * np.max(coeffs[0])

# Apply thresholding to wavelet coefficients
coeffs_compressed = [pywt.threshold(coeff, threshold) for coeff in coeffs]

# Reconstruct the compressed image
image_compressed = pywt.waverec2(coeffs_compressed, 'haar')

# Display the original and compressed images
plt.subplot(1, 2, 1)
plt.imshow(image, cmap='gray')
plt.title('Original Image')
```

```
plt.subplot(1, 2, 2)
plt.imshow(image_compressed, cmap='gray')
plt.title('Compressed Image')

plt.tight_layout()
plt.show()
```

Python provides a wide range of libraries and tools for signal processing tasks. In this tutorial, we explored various aspects of signal processing, including loading and visualizing signals, filtering, Fourier analysis, and wavelet transform. By leveraging these tools, you can perform sophisticated signal processing operations and gain valuable insights from your data. Experiment with different techniques and libraries to further expand your knowledge and expertise in signal processing with Python.

Digital image processing with Python

Image processing is a crucial field in computer science and engineering that deals with the manipulation, enhancement, and analysis of digital images. Images are essential sources of information in various domains, such as computer vision, medical imaging, and remote sensing. Python, with its extensive range of libraries and tools, offers a powerful environment for digital image processing tasks. In this tutorial, we will explore key concepts and demonstrate how to perform digital image processing using Python.

Installing the Required Libraries

Before we delve into digital image processing with Python, let's ensure we have the necessary libraries installed. We will primarily use the following libraries:

NumPy: A fundamental library for numerical computing in Python, providing efficient array operations and linear algebra functions.

pip install numpy

OpenCV: An open-source computer vision library that offers comprehensive image processing and computer vision functions.

pip install opencv-python

Matplotlib: A plotting library that enables us to visualize images and analysis results.

pip install matplotlib

Scikit-image: A library for image processing built on top of NumPy, providing a wide range of image processing algorithms and functions.

pip install scikit-image

Once we have installed these libraries, we can begin our digital image processing tasks.

Loading and Displaying Images

Before processing images, we need to load and display them. Python provides various methods to load images, depending on the image format. Let's consider an example where we have an image file in JPEG format. We can use the OpenCV library to load and display the image:

```
import cv2
import matplotlib.pyplot as plt
```

```
# Load the image
image = cv2.imread('image.jpg')

# Display the image
plt.imshow(cv2.cvtColor(image, cv2.COLOR_BGR2RGB))
plt.axis('off')
plt.show()
```

Image Filtering and Enhancement

Filtering and enhancement operations are vital in image processing to remove noise, improve image quality, and highlight important features. In Python, we can apply various filters and enhancement techniques using the OpenCV and scikit-image libraries. Let's consider an example where we apply a Gaussian blur filter and contrast enhancement to an image:

```
from skimage import filters
from skimage.exposure import rescale_intensity

# Apply Gaussian blur
blurred_image = cv2.GaussianBlur(image, (5, 5), 0)

# Apply contrast enhancement
enhanced_image = rescale_intensity(image, in_range='image', out_range=np.uint8)

# Display the original, blurred, and enhanced images
plt.subplot(1, 3, 1)
plt.imshow(cv2.cvtColor(image, cv2.COLOR_BGR2RGB))
plt.axis('off')
plt.title('Original Image')

plt.subplot(1, 3, 2)
plt.imshow(cv2.cvtColor(blurred_image, cv2.COLOR_BGR2RGB))
plt.axis('off')
plt.title('Blurred Image')

plt.subplot(1, 3, 3)
plt.imshow(cv2.cvtColor(enhanced_image, cv2.COLOR_BGR2RGB))
plt.axis('off')
plt.title('Enhanced Image')

plt.tight_layout()
plt.show()
```

Image Segmentation

Image segmentation involves partitioning an image into distinct regions based on their properties or characteristics. It is a crucial step in various image analysis tasks, such as object detection and image understanding. Python provides several algorithms and techniques for image segmentation. Let's consider an example where we perform image segmentation using the k-means clustering algorithm:

```python
from sklearn.cluster import KMeans

# Reshape the image into a 2D array
pixel_values = image.reshape((-1, 3))


# Apply k-means clustering
kmeans = KMeans(n_clusters=3)
kmeans.fit(pixel_values)

# Get the cluster labels
labels = kmeans.labels_

# Reshape the labels back into the original image shape
segmented_image = labels.reshape(image.shape[:2])

# Display the original and segmented images
plt.subplot(1, 2, 1)
plt.imshow(cv2.cvtColor(image, cv2.COLOR_BGR2RGB))
plt.axis('off')
plt.title('Original Image')

plt.subplot(1, 2, 2)
plt.imshow(segmented_image, cmap='viridis')
plt.axis('off')
plt.title('Segmented Image')

plt.tight_layout()
plt.show()
```

Image Feature Extraction

Feature extraction aims to identify and extract meaningful information or features from images. These features can be used for various purposes, such as image classification, object recognition, and image retrieval. Python offers numerous techniques for image feature extraction, including popular algorithms such as SIFT (Scale-Invariant Feature Transform) and SURF (Speeded Up Robust Features). Let's consider an example where we extract and visualize SIFT features from an image using the OpenCV library:

```python
# Convert the image to grayscale
gray_image = cv2.cvtColor(image, cv2.COLOR_BGR2GRAY)

# Initialize the SIFT feature extractor
sift = cv2.SIFT_create()

# Detect and compute SIFT features
keypoints, descriptors = sift.detectAndCompute(gray_image, None)

# Visualize the detected keypoints
sift_image = cv2.drawKeypoints(gray_image, keypoints, None)

# Display the original image and the SIFT features
plt.subplot(1, 2, 1)
plt.imshow(cv2.cvtColor(image, cv2.COLOR_BGR2RGB))
plt.axis('off')
plt.title('Original Image')

plt.subplot(1, 2, 2)
plt.imshow(cv2.cvtColor(sift_image, cv2.COLOR_BGR2RGB))
plt.axis('off')
plt.title('SIFT Features')

plt.tight_layout()
plt.show()
```

Python provides a wide range of libraries and tools for digital image processing tasks. In this tutorial, we explored various aspects of image processing, including loading and displaying images, filtering and enhancement, segmentation, and feature extraction. By leveraging these tools and techniques, you can perform advanced image analysis tasks and gain valuable insights from your images. Experiment with different algorithms and libraries to further expand your knowledge and expertise in digital image processing with Python.

GUI programming with Tkinter in Python

GUI (Graphical User Interface) programming involves creating visual interfaces for applications, allowing users to interact with them using graphical elements such as buttons, menus, and forms. Python provides several libraries for GUI development, and one of the most popular and widely used is Tkinter. Tkinter is a built-in library in Python that enables developers to create intuitive and interactive graphical interfaces. In this tutorial, we will explore the basics of GUI programming with Tkinter and demonstrate how to build simple GUI applications using Python.

Installing Tkinter

Tkinter is included with Python by default, so there is no need for separate installation. However, you may need to ensure that Tkinter is installed and available on your system. To check if Tkinter is installed, open a Python interpreter and type the following:

import tkinter

If the import statement does not produce an error, then Tkinter is already installed. Otherwise, you can install Tkinter using the following command:

pip install tkinter

Once Tkinter is installed, we can proceed with GUI programming in Python.

Creating a Basic GUI Window

Let's start by creating a basic GUI window using Tkinter. The window serves as the main container for all the graphical elements of our application. Here's an example that creates a simple window with a title and size:

```python
import tkinter as tk

# Create a window
window = tk.Tk()

# Set the window title
window.title("My GUI App")

# Set the window size
window.geometry("400x300")

# Start the main event loop
window.mainloop()
```

Adding Widgets to the GUI

Widgets are the building blocks of a GUI application. They are the visual elements such as buttons, labels, text boxes, and checkboxes that users interact with. We can add various types of widgets to our GUI window using Tkinter. Here's an example that adds a button and a label to the window:

```python
import tkinter as tk

# Create a window
window = tk.Tk()
window.title("My GUI App")
window.geometry("400x300")

# Create a button
button = tk.Button(window, text="Click Me!")

# Create a label
label = tk.Label(window, text="Hello, World!")

# Add the button and label to the window
button.pack()
label.pack()

# Start the main event loop
window.mainloop()
```

Handling Widget Events

Widgets can trigger events, such as button clicks or text entry. We can define functions that handle these events and perform specific actions when they occur. Here's an example that adds a button to the window and defines a function to handle the button click event:

```python
import tkinter as tk

# Create a window
window = tk.Tk()
window.title("My GUI App")
window.geometry("400x300")

# Define a function to handle button clicks
def button_click():
    print("Button clicked!")

# Create a button and bind it to the button_click function
button = tk.Button(window, text="Click Me!", command=button_click)
button.pack()
```

```
# Start the main event loop
window.mainloop()
```

Adding Layout Management

Layout management is essential for arranging widgets within a window. Tkinter provides various layout managers, such as pack, grid, and place, to control the positioning and resizing of widgets. Here's an example that demonstrates the use of the pack layout manager to position widgets:

```
import tkinter as tk

# Create a window
window = tk.Tk()
window.title("My GUI App")
window.geometry("400x300")

# Create three buttons
button1 = tk.Button(window, text="Button 1")
button2 = tk.Button(window, text="

"Button 2")
button3 = tk.Button(window, text="Button 3")

Pack the buttons horizontally
button1.pack(side=tk.LEFT)
button2.pack(side=tk.LEFT)
button3.pack(side=tk.LEFT)

Start the main event loop
window.mainloop()

"Button 2")
button3 = tk.Button(window, text="Button 3")

Pack the buttons horizontally
button1.pack(side=tk.LEFT)
button2.pack(side=tk.LEFT)
button3.pack(side=tk.LEFT)

Start the main event loop
window.mainloop()
```

Tkinter provides a straightforward and powerful way to create GUI applications in Python. In this tutorial, we explored the basics of GUI programming with Tkinter, including creating a window, adding widgets, handling events, managing layouts, and incorporating user input and output. With Tkinter's extensive set of features and flexibility, you can create interactive and user-friendly applications tailored to your specific needs. Experiment with different widgets, event handling techniques, and layout managers to further enhance your GUI programming skills with Python and Tkinter.

GUI programming with PyQt in Python

Introduction to GUI Programming
GUI (Graphical User Interface) programming involves creating visual interfaces for applications, enabling users to interact with them using graphical elements such as buttons, menus, and forms. Python provides several libraries for GUI development, and one of the popular choices is PyQt. PyQt is a Python binding for the Qt framework, which is a powerful and versatile GUI toolkit. In this tutorial, we will explore the basics of GUI programming with PyQt and demonstrate how to build GUI applications using Python.

Installing PyQt

Before we begin GUI programming with PyQt, we need to install the library. PyQt can be installed using pip, the Python package manager. Open a terminal or command prompt and execute the following command:

pip install pyqt5

Once PyQt is installed, we can proceed with GUI programming in Python.

Creating a Basic GUI Window
Let's start by creating a basic GUI window using PyQt. The window serves as the main container for all the graphical elements of our application. Here's an example that creates a simple window with a title and size:

```
import sys
from PyQt5.QtWidgets import QApplication, QMainWindow

# Create the application
app = QApplication(sys.argv)

# Create the main window
window = QMainWindow()
window.setWindowTitle("My GUI App")
window.setGeometry(100, 100, 400, 300)

# Show the window
window.show()

# Execute the application's event loop
sys.exit(app.exec())
```

Adding Widgets to the GUI

Widgets are the building blocks of a GUI application. They are the visual elements such as buttons, labels, text boxes, and checkboxes that users interact with. We can add various types of widgets to our GUI window using PyQt. Here's an example that adds a button and a label to the window:

```python
import sys
from PyQt5.QtWidgets import QApplication, QMainWindow, QPushButton, QLabel

# Create the application
app = QApplication(sys.argv)

# Create the main window
window = QMainWindow()
window.setWindowTitle("My GUI App")
window.setGeometry(100, 100, 400, 300)

# Create a button
button = QPushButton("Click Me!", window)
button.setGeometry(100, 100, 100, 30)

# Create a label
label = QLabel("Hello, World!", window)
label.setGeometry(100, 150, 200, 30)

# Show the window
window.show()

# Execute the application's event loop
sys.exit(app.exec())
```

Handling Widget Events

Widgets can trigger events, such as button clicks or text entry. We can define functions that handle these events and perform specific actions when they occur. Here's an example that adds a button to the window and defines a function to handle the button click event:

```python
import sys
from PyQt5.QtWidgets import QApplication, QMainWindow, QPushButton

# Create the application
app = QApplication(sys.argv)

# Create the main window
window = QMainWindow()
window.setWindowTitle("My GUI App")
window.setGeometry(100, 100, 400, 300)
```

```
# Define a function to handle button clicks
def button_click():
    print("Button clicked!")

# Create a button and connect it to the button_click function
button = QPushButton("Click Me!", window)
button.setGeometry(100, 100, 100, 30)
button.clicked.connect(button_click)

# Show the window
window.show()

# Execute the application's event loop
sys.exit(app.exec())
```

Adding Layout Management

Layout management is essential for arranging widgets within a window. PyQt provides various layout managers, such as QVBoxLayout, QHBoxLayout, and QGridLayout, to control the positioning and resizing of widgets. Here's an example that demonstrates the use of QVBoxLayout to position widgets vertically:

```
import sys
from PyQt5.QtWidgets import QApplication, QMainWindow, QVBoxLayout, QPushButton, QLabel, QWidget

# Create the application
app = QApplication(sys.argv)

# Create the main window
window = QMainWindow()
window.setWindowTitle("My GUI App")
window.setGeometry(100, 100, 400, 300)

# Create a widget to hold the layout
widget = QWidget(window)

# Create a vertical layout
layout = QVBoxLayout(widget)

# Create a button
button1 = QPushButton("Button 1")
button2 = QPushButton("Button 2")
button3 = QPushButton("Button 3")

# Create a label
label = QLabel("Hello, World!")
```

```
# Add the widgets to the layout
layout.addWidget(button1)
layout.addWidget(button2)
layout.addWidget(button3)
layout.addWidget(label)

# Set the layout for the widget
widget.setLayout(layout)

# Set the widget as the central widget of the window
window.setCentralWidget(widget)

# Show the window
window.show()

# Execute the application's event loop
sys.exit(app.exec())
```

Adding User Input and Output

GUI applications often require user input and provide output to the user. PyQt offers various widgets for handling input and displaying output, such as QLineEdit and QMessageBox. Here's an example that adds a QLineEdit widget for user input and a QMessageBox for displaying output:

```
import sys
from PyQt5.QtWidgets import QApplication, QMainWindow, QVBoxLayout, QPushButton,
QLabel, QLineEdit, QMessageBox, QWidget

# Create the application
app = QApplication(sys.argv)

# Create the main window
window = QMainWindow()
window.setWindowTitle("My GUI App")
window.setGeometry(100, 100, 400, 300)

# Create a widget to hold the layout
widget = QWidget(window)

# Create a vertical layout
layout = QVBoxLayout(widget)

# Create a line edit for user input
input_box = QLineEdit()

# Create a button and connect it to a function for displaying output
button = QPushButton("Show Message")
```

```python
def show_message():
    user_input = input_box.text()
    QMessageBox.information(window, "Message", f"Entered text: {user_input}")

button.clicked.connect(show_message)

# Add the input box and button to the layout
layout.addWidget(input_box)
layout.addWidget(button)

# Set the layout for the widget
widget.setLayout(layout)

# Set the widget as the central widget of the window
window.setCentralWidget(widget)

# Show the window
window.show()

# Execute the application's event loop
sys.exit(app.exec())
```

PyQt provides a robust and feature-rich toolkit for GUI programming in Python. In this tutorial, we explored the basics of GUI programming with PyQt, including creating a window, adding widgets, handling events, managing layouts, and incorporating user input and output. PyQt's extensive capabilities and Qt's versatility allow you to create interactive and visually appealing applications tailored to your specific requirements. Experiment with different widgets, layout managers, and event handling techniques to further enhance your GUI programming skills with Python and PyQt.

Introduction to web scraping libraries (BeautifulSoup, Scrapy, etc.)

Web Scraping Libraries: Introduction

Web scraping is the process of extracting data from websites. It allows us to automate data collection, gather information, and perform various tasks such as data analysis, content aggregation, and monitoring. Python offers several powerful libraries for web scraping, including BeautifulSoup, Scrapy, and more. In this tutorial, we will provide an overview of these popular web scraping libraries and demonstrate their usage in Python.

BeautifulSoup: Extracting Data from HTML

BeautifulSoup is a Python library that makes it easy to scrape information from HTML and XML documents. It provides a simple and intuitive interface to navigate and search the HTML structure, extract data from tags, and handle different types of data parsing. Here's an example that demonstrates the basic usage of BeautifulSoup:

```python
from bs4 import BeautifulSoup
import requests

# Send a request to the webpage
response = requests.get('https://example.com')

# Create a BeautifulSoup object
soup = BeautifulSoup(response.text, 'html.parser')

# Find and print the page title
title = soup.find('title').text
print(f"Page Title: {title}")

# Find and print all the links on the page
links = soup.find_all('a')
for link in links:
    print(link['href'])
```

Scrapy: Powerful Web Scraping Framework

Scrapy is a powerful and flexible web scraping framework for Python. It provides a high-level API for efficiently extracting data from websites, handling requests and responses, and following links. Scrapy is well-suited for large-scale scraping projects and offers advanced features such as automated session management, caching, and item pipelines. Here's an example that demonstrates how to create a basic Scrapy spider:

231

```
import scrapy

class MySpider(scrapy.Spider):
    name = 'example_spider'
    start_urls = ['https://example.com']

    def parse(self, response):
        # Extract data from the page
        title = response.css('title::text').get()
        links = response.css('a::attr(href)').getall()

        # Print the extracted data
        print(f"Page Title: {title}")
        print("Links:")
        for link in links:
            print(link)
```

To run the Scrapy spider, save the code in a file and execute the following command in the terminal:

scrapy runspider filename.py

Other Web Scraping Libraries

Apart from BeautifulSoup and Scrapy, there are several other web scraping libraries available in Python, each with its own strengths and features. Some notable mentions include:

Selenium: A library for automating web browsers, useful for scraping websites with dynamic content or interacting with JavaScript-based functionality.
Requests-HTML: A library built on top of requests that simplifies web scraping by combining the features of requests, BeautifulSoup, and Selenium.
PyQuery: A jQuery-like library for parsing HTML and XML documents, providing a familiar syntax for selecting and manipulating elements.

Web scraping is a valuable technique for extracting data from websites, and Python offers a range of powerful libraries to facilitate the process. In this tutorial, we introduced BeautifulSoup and Scrapy, two popular web scraping libraries in Python. We also mentioned other libraries such as Selenium, Requests-HTML, and PyQuery that can be useful for specific scraping requirements. By leveraging these libraries, you can efficiently scrape websites, gather data, and automate repetitive tasks, enabling you to extract valuable insights and streamline your data analysis workflow.

Scraping dynamic web pages with Python

Introduction to Dynamic Web Pages
Dynamic web pages are websites that generate content dynamically through JavaScript or Ajax requests. Unlike static web pages, which have fixed HTML content, dynamic web pages load and display data in real-time, often interacting with users. When it comes to web scraping, extracting data from dynamic web pages requires a different approach. In this tutorial, we will explore techniques and Python libraries to scrape dynamic web pages effectively.

Understanding the Basics

Before diving into dynamic web scraping, let's briefly cover the fundamental concepts and tools involved:

1. HTML Parsing: HTML parsing is the process of analyzing the HTML structure of a web page to extract relevant data. Python provides various libraries for parsing HTML, such as BeautifulSoup and lxml.

2. Web Drivers: Web drivers, such as Selenium WebDriver, simulate real web browsers to interact with dynamic web pages. They automate actions like clicking buttons, submitting forms, and waiting for dynamic content to load.

3. JavaScript Rendering: Dynamic web pages often rely on JavaScript to load and update content. To scrape dynamic pages, we need to ensure that the JavaScript code is executed to fetch the desired data. This can be achieved by using headless browsers or browser automation tools.

Scraping Dynamic Web Pages with Selenium

Selenium is a popular Python library for web automation and scraping dynamic web pages. It allows us to control web browsers programmatically, enabling interaction with JavaScript-based content. Here's an example that demonstrates how to scrape a dynamic web page using Selenium:

```
from selenium import webdriver

# Set up the Selenium WebDriver (Make sure to install the appropriate driver for your browser)
driver = webdriver.Chrome()

# Load the web page
driver.get('https://example.com')

# Wait for dynamic content to load (optional)
# Note: Use explicit or implicit waits to ensure the page has finished rendering
```

```
# Extract data from the web page
data = driver.find_element_by_xpath('//span[@class="dynamic-data"]').text
print(f"Dynamic Data: {data}")

# Close the browser
driver.quit()
```

Scraping Dynamic Web Pages with Scrapy-Selenium

Scrapy is a powerful web scraping framework, and Scrapy-Selenium is a Scrapy middleware that combines Scrapy with Selenium WebDriver. This integration allows us to scrape dynamic web pages efficiently. Here's an example of scraping a dynamic web page using Scrapy-Selenium:

```
import scrapy
from scrapy_selenium import SeleniumRequest

class MySpider(scrapy.Spider):
    name = 'dynamic_spider'
    start_urls = ['https://example.com']

    def start_requests(self):
        for url in self.start_urls:
            yield SeleniumRequest(url=url, callback=self.parse)

    def parse(self, response):
        # Extract data from the dynamic web page
        data = response.xpath('//span[@class="dynamic-data"]').get()
        print(f"Dynamic Data: {data}")
```

To run the Scrapy spider with Scrapy-Selenium, save the code in a file and execute the following command in the terminal:

```
scrapy crawl dynamic_spider
```

Alternative Approaches

Apart from Selenium and Scrapy-Selenium, there are other tools and approaches you can consider for scraping dynamic web pages:

1. Splash: Splash is a JavaScript rendering service with an HTTP API. It provides a headless browser environment to render and scrape JavaScript-based content.

2. Puppeteer: Puppeteer is a Node.js library that provides a high-level API to control headless Chrome or Chromium browsers. It allows scraping dynamic pages with JavaScript rendering.

Scraping dynamic web pages requires additional techniques compared to static pages. By leveraging Python libraries like Selenium and Scrapy-Selenium, we can interact with JavaScript-based content and extract data

Advanced web development with Flask

Flask is a popular microframework for web development in Python. It provides a simple yet powerful foundation for building web applications. In this tutorial, we will explore advanced techniques and features of Flask to take your web development skills to the next level. From creating RESTful APIs to implementing authentication and deploying Flask applications, we will cover a range of topics that will help you build robust and scalable web applications.

Creating RESTful APIs with Flask

RESTful APIs allow applications to communicate and exchange data over the web using standard HTTP methods. Flask provides a flexible framework for building RESTful APIs. Here's an example that demonstrates how to create a simple API endpoint using Flask:

```python
from flask import Flask, jsonify

app = Flask(__name__)

@app.route('/api/hello', methods=['GET'])
def hello():
    data = {'message': 'Hello, API!'}
    return jsonify(data)

if __name__ == '__main__':
    app.run()
```

Implementing Authentication with Flask

Authentication is a critical aspect of web applications to ensure secure access and protect sensitive data. Flask provides extensions and libraries to implement authentication mechanisms easily. One popular library is Flask-Login. Here's an example that shows how to integrate Flask-Login for user authentication:

```python
from flask import Flask, render_template, redirect, url_for
from flask_login import LoginManager, login_user, login_required

app = Flask(__name__)
app.secret_key = 'your_secret_key'

login_manager = LoginManager(app)

# Define User model and user_loader callback function
```

```python
@login_manager.user_loader
def load_user(user_id):
    # Load and return User object based on user_id
    pass

@app.route('/login', methods=['GET', 'POST'])
def login():
    # Handle user login logic
    pass

@app.route('/dashboard')
@login_required
def dashboard():
    # Protected route accessible only for authenticated users
    pass

if __name__ == '__main__':
    app.run()
```

Database Integration with Flask

Web applications often require persistent data storage. Flask integrates seamlessly with various databases, allowing you to interact with data using ORM (Object-Relational Mapping) libraries such as SQLAlchemy. Here's an example that demonstrates how to connect Flask with a SQLite database using SQLAlchemy:

```python
from flask import Flask
from flask_sqlalchemy import SQLAlchemy

app = Flask(__name__)
app.config['SQLALCHEMY_DATABASE_URI'] = 'sqlite:///mydatabase.db'
db = SQLAlchemy(app)

# Define models and create database tables

class User(db.Model):
    id = db.Column(db.Integer, primary_key=True)
    name = db.Column(db.String(50), nullable=False)
    email = db.Column(db.String(50), unique=True, nullable=False)

if __name__ == '__main__':
    app.run()
```

Deploying Flask Applications

Once your Flask application is ready, you need to deploy it to make it accessible to users. There are several deployment options available, including hosting on cloud platforms, deploying to virtual private servers, or using containerization technologies like Docker. Here's a brief overview of the deployment process:

1. Prepare your application for production by configuring environment variables, updating database connections, and securing sensitive information.

2. Choose a deployment platform such as Heroku, AWS, or Google Cloud Platform. Follow their documentation to set up the necessary infrastructure and deploy your Flask application.

3. Consider using WSGI servers like Gunicorn or uWSGI to handle incoming requests and serve your Flask application.

4. Configure SSL/TLS certificates to enable secure communication over HTTPS.

Flask provides a powerful foundation for advanced web development in Python. In this tutorial, we explored creating RESTful APIs, implementing authentication, integrating databases, and deploying Flask

Advanced web development with Django

Django is a powerful web development framework that allows developers to build robust and scalable web applications. In this guide, we will explore advanced techniques and concepts in Django that will take your web development skills to the next level. From handling complex database relationships to implementing secure authentication and authorization mechanisms, we will cover various aspects of advanced web development using Python and Django.

Setting Up Your Django Project

Before diving into advanced concepts, let's start by setting up a new Django project. Open your terminal or command prompt and navigate to the desired directory where you want to create your project. Then, run the following commands:

```
$ pip install Django
$ django-admin startproject myproject
$ cd myproject
$ python manage.py runserver
```

Introduction to Advanced Web Development with Django

Django is a powerful web development framework that allows developers to build robust and scalable web applications. In this guide, we will explore advanced techniques and concepts in Django that will take your web development skills to the next level. From handling complex database relationships to implementing secure authentication and authorization mechanisms, we will cover various aspects of advanced web development using Python and Django.

Setting Up Your Django Project

Before diving into advanced concepts, let's start by setting up a new Django project. Open your terminal or command prompt and navigate to the desired directory where you want to create your project. Then, run the following commands:

```
$ pip install Django
$ django-admin startproject myproject
$ cd myproject
$ python manage.py runserver
```

This will create a new Django project called "myproject" and start a local development server. You can access your project by opening your browser and navigating to http://localhost:8000/.

Working with Complex Database Relationships

One of Django's strengths is its robust Object-Relational Mapping (ORM) system, which simplifies working with databases. In advanced web development, you often encounter complex database relationships, such as many-to-many or one-to-many relationships. Django provides powerful tools to handle these scenarios effortlessly.

To define a many-to-many relationship between two models, you can use the ManyToManyField field in your Django model. For example, consider a scenario where a User can have multiple Books:

```python
from django.db import models

class User(models.Model):
    name = models.CharField(max_length=100)
    books = models.ManyToManyField(Book)

class Book(models.Model):
    title = models.CharField(max_length=100)
```

With this setup, you can easily access a user's books or find users who have a specific book associated with them. Django takes care of creating the necessary database tables and provides a convenient API to perform complex queries.

Implementing Secure Authentication and Authorization

In any web application, user authentication and authorization are crucial aspects of security. Django provides a robust authentication system out-of-the-box, making it easier to implement secure login and registration functionality.

To enable authentication in your Django project, you need to configure the authentication backend and define a user model. Django provides a default user model, but you can also create a custom user model to suit your application's specific requirements.

Once you have set up authentication, you can control access to different parts of your application using Django's authorization system. By defining permissions and roles, you can restrict certain views or actions to authorized users only.

Integrating Frontend Frameworks

While Django provides powerful backend capabilities, you might want to enhance your application's frontend with a modern JavaScript framework like React or Vue.js. Django seamlessly integrates with frontend frameworks, allowing you to build Single-Page Applications (SPAs) or enhance specific parts of your application with dynamic interactivity.

To integrate a frontend framework, you can use Django's built-in template engine or create a RESTful API using Django's views and serializers. The frontend framework can then communicate with the Django backend through API endpoints, fetching and updating data asynchronously.

Deploying Your Django Application

After developing your advanced Django application, it's time to deploy it to a production environment. Django supports various deployment options, including deploying to traditional servers, cloud platforms like AWS or Google Cloud, or using Platform-as-a-Service (PaaS) providers like Heroku.

When deploying your Django application, consider optimizing your code for performance, configuring caching mechanisms, setting up secure HTTPS connections, and ensuring proper database management.

In this guide, we have explored advanced web development techniques with Django. From managing complex database relationships to implementing secure authentication and integrating frontend frameworks, Django provides a comprehensive toolkit for building robust web

Building RESTful APIs with Python and Flask

Building RESTful APIs using Python and Flask is a powerful way to create scalable and flexible web services. REST (Representational State Transfer) is an architectural style that allows clients to interact with server resources through standard HTTP methods. Flask, a lightweight web framework for Python, provides a simple and elegant solution for building RESTful APIs.

Setting Up Your Flask Project

To get started, you need to set up a Flask project. Open your terminal or command prompt and navigate to the desired directory where you want to create your project. Then, run the following commands:

```
$ pip install Flask
$ mkdir myproject
$ cd myproject
$ touch app.py
```

This will install Flask and create a new directory called "myproject" with a file named "app.py" to hold your Flask application code.

Defining Routes and Handling Requests

In Flask, routes define the URL patterns that your API will respond to. You can define routes using decorators provided by Flask, such as @app.route('/endpoint'). Within the route functions, you can handle different HTTP methods like GET, POST, PUT, and DELETE to perform the appropriate actions.

Here's an example of a simple Flask route that handles a GET request:

```
from flask import Flask

app = Flask(__name__)

@app.route('/api/users', methods=['GET'])
def get_users():
    # Code to fetch and return a list of users
    return 'Response containing users'
```

With this setup, when a GET request is made to the '/api/users' endpoint, the get_users function will be executed, and you can implement the logic to fetch the list of users from a database or any other data source.

Working with Request Data and Parameters

In a RESTful API, clients often send data as part of the request payload or as URL parameters. Flask provides convenient methods to access this data within your route functions.

To access request data sent in the payload, you can use the request.json attribute, which provides a dictionary-like interface to the JSON data. For example:

```
from flask import Flask, request

app = Flask(__name__)

@app.route('/api/users', methods=['POST'])
def create_user():
    user_data = request.json
    # Code to create a new user using the user_data
    return 'User created successfully'
```

You can also access URL parameters using Flask's variable rules. Simply specify the parameter name within angled brackets in the route decorator and access it as an argument in your route function. For example:

```
@app.route('/api/users/<user_id>', methods=['GET'])
def get_user(user_id):
    # Code to fetch and return a specific user based on user_id
    return 'Response containing user details'
```

Serializing and Deserializing Data

When working with RESTful APIs, it's common to serialize and deserialize data between the API and the client. Serialization refers to converting Python objects to a format like JSON, while deserialization converts the data back to Python objects.

Flask provides various libraries and tools to handle serialization and deserialization. One popular library is Flask-RESTful, which extends Flask to simplify building APIs. It provides features like request parsing, response formatting, and input validation.

To use Flask-RESTful, you need to install it using pip and then define resources that represent different API endpoints. Each resource can handle multiple HTTP methods and encapsulate the necessary logic for data processing.

Handling Authentication and Authorization

Authentication and authorization are critical aspects of building secure APIs. Flask provides several extensions and libraries to handle these functionalities effectively.

One popular library is Flask-JWT, which enables JSON Web Token (JWT) authentication in your Flask application. JSON Web Tokens are a secure way to transmit authentication information between the client and the server.

To use Flask-JWT, you need to install it using pip and configure it in your Flask application. You can define protected routes that require authentication by applying the @jwt_required decorator to your route functions. For example:

```python
from flask import Flask
from flask_jwt import JWT, jwt_required

app = Flask(__name__)
app.config['SECRET_KEY'] = 'your_secret_key_here'

# JWT configuration
def authenticate(username, password):
    # Code to authenticate the user
    return User(username)

def identity(payload):
    user_id = payload['identity']
    # Code to fetch the user based on user_id
    return User(user_id)

jwt = JWT(app, authenticate, identity)

@app.route('/api/protected', methods=['GET'])
@jwt_required()
def protected_route():
    # Code to handle the protected route
    return 'Protected route response'
```

In this example, the authenticate function is responsible for validating the user's credentials, while the identity function retrieves the user's information based on the payload extracted from the JWT. The @jwt_required() decorator ensures that the user must provide a valid JWT to access the protected route.

Error Handling and Response Formatting

When developing APIs, it's essential to provide meaningful error messages and format the responses consistently. Flask allows you to handle errors and format responses using its error handling mechanism.

You can define custom error handlers to handle specific HTTP error codes or exceptions. For example:

```python
from flask import Flask, jsonify

app = Flask(__name__)

@app.errorhandler(404)
def not_found_error(error):
    return jsonify({'error': 'Not found'}), 404

@app.errorhandler(500)
def internal_server_error(error):
    return jsonify({'error': 'Internal server error'}), 500
```

In this code snippet, the not_found_error function handles the 404 error code, and the internal_server_error function handles the 500 error code. These functions return a JSON response with an appropriate error message.

Additionally, you can format your API responses using the jsonify function provided by Flask. This function serializes Python dictionaries into JSON responses with the correct content-type header.

Testing Your API

Testing is a crucial part of developing robust APIs. Flask provides a testing framework that allows you to write unit tests for your API endpoints.

You can use the Flask.testing module to simulate HTTP requests and assert the expected responses. This allows you to verify that your routes handle different HTTP methods correctly, handle request data, and return the expected results.

Here's an example of a simple unit test using Flask's testing framework:

```python
import unittest
from app import app

class APITestCase(unittest.TestCase):
    def setUp(self):
```

```
        self.app = app.test_client()

    def test_get_users(self):
        response = self.app.get('/api/users')
        self.assertEqual(response.status_code, 200)
        self.assertEqual(response.get_json(), {'users': []})

if __name__ == '__main__':
    unittest.main()
```

In this test case, we create an instance of the Flask test client and use it to make a GET request to the '/api/users' endpoint. We then assert that the response status code is 200 (indicating a successful request) and check the JSON response body.

In this guide, we have explored the process of building RESTful APIs with Python and Flask. From setting up a Flask project and defining routes to handling requests, authentication, and error handling, Flask provides a flexible and intuitive framework for developing powerful APIs.

Building RESTful APIs with Python and Django

Building RESTful APIs using Python and Django is a robust and efficient way to create scalable and feature-rich web services. Django, a high-level Python web framework, provides a comprehensive set of tools and conventions that make API development straightforward and secure. In this guide, we will explore the process of building RESTful APIs with Python and Django.

Setting Up Your Django Project

To begin, you need to set up a Django project for your API. Open your terminal or command prompt and navigate to the desired directory where you want to create your project. Then, run the following commands:

```
$ pip install Django
$ django-admin startproject myproject
$ cd myproject
```

This will install Django and create a new Django project called "myproject". You can then proceed to create a new Django app within your project, specifically for your API functionality.

Defining Models for Your API Resources

In Django, models represent the data structure of your application. To build an API, you need to define models that represent your API resources. These models will be responsible for interacting with the database and providing a structured representation of your data.

For example, suppose you are building an API for a blog application. You may define a Post model as follows:

```python
from django.db import models

class Post(models.Model):
    title = models.CharField(max_length=100)
    content = models.TextField()
    created_at = models.DateTimeField(auto_now_add=True)
```

With this model, you can create, retrieve, update, and delete blog posts through your API.

Implementing API Views and Serializers

In Django, views handle incoming requests and return appropriate responses. For building RESTful APIs, Django provides the APIView class, which simplifies the implementation of API views.

To create an API view, you subclass the APIView class and define methods that correspond to different HTTP methods. For example, to handle GET and POST requests for the Post resource, you can create a view as follows:

```python
from rest_framework.views import APIView
from rest_framework.response import Response

class PostView(APIView):
    def get(self, request):
        posts = Post.objects.all()
        serializer = PostSerializer(posts, many=True)
        return Response(serializer.data)

    def post(self, request):
        serializer = PostSerializer(data=request.data)
        if serializer.is_valid():
            serializer.save()
            return Response(serializer.data, status=201)
        return Response(serializer.errors, status=400)
```

In this example, the get method retrieves all the posts from the database and serializes them using a PostSerializer. The post method creates a new post by deserializing the request data and saving it.

To handle serialization and deserialization, Django provides the Serializer class. You define a serializer that specifies the fields you want to include in the API representation of your model. For our Post model, a serializer may look like this:

```python
from rest_framework import serializers

class PostSerializer(serializers.ModelSerializer):
    class Meta:
        model = Post
        fields = ['id', 'title', 'content', 'created_at']
```

Configuring URL Routing for Your API

URL routing maps incoming requests to the appropriate view functions in Django. To configure URL routing for your API, you need to define URL patterns in your Django project's urls.py file.

You can create a separate urls.py file specifically for your API or include your API URLs within the project-level urls.py file. Here's an example of including API URLs within the project-level file:

```
from django.urls import path, include

urlpatterns = [
    # Other URL patterns for your project

path('api/', include('api.urls')),
# Other URL patterns for your project
]
```

In this example, the `include` function is used to include the URLs defined in the `api.urls` module, which will handle API-specific routing.

Within the `api.urls` module, you can define URL patterns for your API views. For example:

```
from django.urls import path
from .views import PostView

urlpatterns = [
    path('posts/', PostView.as_view(), name='post-list'),
    # Other URL patterns for your API views
]
```

In this case, the URL pattern /posts/ maps to the PostView API view, allowing you to perform CRUD operations on blog posts.

Adding Authentication and Permissions

Securing your API is essential, and Django provides various authentication and permission options. You can choose from built-in authentication schemes like token authentication or integrate with popular authentication libraries like Django REST Framework's authentication classes.

To add authentication, you can specify authentication classes in your Django settings. For example, to enable token authentication:

```
REST_FRAMEWORK = {
    'DEFAULT_AUTHENTICATION_CLASSES': [
        'rest_framework.authentication.TokenAuthentication',
        # Other authentication classes
    ],
    'DEFAULT_PERMISSION_CLASSES': [
        'rest_framework.permissions.IsAuthenticated',
        # Other permission classes
    ],
}
```

By default, the IsAuthenticated permission class ensures that only authenticated users can access your API endpoints. You can customize permissions based on your specific requirements.

Testing Your API

Testing your API ensures its functionality and helps catch errors early in the development process. Django provides a testing framework that allows you to write unit tests for your API views and other components.

You can create test cases by subclassing Django's TestCase and using various testing utilities provided by Django, such as the Client class. Here's an example of a test case for the PostView API view:

```
from django.test import TestCase
from rest_framework.test import APIClient

class PostViewTestCase(TestCase):
    def setUp(self):
        self.client = APIClient()

    def test_get_posts(self):
        response = self.client.get('/api/posts/')
        self.assertEqual(response.status_code, 200)

    def test_create_post(self):
        data = {'title': 'New Post', 'content': 'This is a new post'}
        response = self.client.post('/api/posts/', data)
        self.assertEqual(response.status_code, 201)
```

In this example, the test_get_posts method tests the GET request to retrieve all posts, while the test_create_post method tests the POST request to create a new post. Assertions are used to verify the response status codes.

In this guide, we explored the process of building RESTful APIs with Python and Django. By leveraging the powerful features of Django, such as models, views, serializers, and URL routing, you can easily create robust and feature-rich APIs. Additionally, Django's authentication and testing frameworks help ensure the security and functionality of your API.

Building real-time web applications with Python and WebSockets

Building real-time web applications with Python and WebSockets can be an exciting and powerful endeavor. WebSockets are a communication protocol that enables bidirectional and real-time communication between web clients and servers. By leveraging Python's robust capabilities and the flexibility of WebSockets, developers can create dynamic and interactive web applications that provide seamless user experiences.

To get started, you'll need to set up a Python environment and install the necessary packages. Python provides several WebSocket libraries, such as websockets, Tornado, and Socket.IO, which you can choose based on your specific requirements. For this example, let's use the websockets library, which is a lightweight and easy-to-use option.

First, you need to install the websockets library using pip:

pip install websockets

Once installed, you can begin building your real-time web application. Let's outline the general steps involved:

Import the necessary modules:

```
import asyncio
import websockets
```

Create an asynchronous function to handle incoming WebSocket connections:

```
async def handle_websocket(websocket, path):
    # Logic to handle incoming messages and send responses
    pass
```

Start the WebSocket server and bind it to a specific host and port:

```
start_server = websockets.serve(handle_websocket, 'localhost', 8000)

async def main():
    async with start_server:
        await start_server.serve_forever()

asyncio.run(main())
```

With these steps in place, you have a basic WebSocket server up and running. However, to make it truly interactive, you'll need to handle incoming messages and send responses.

To handle incoming messages, you can add logic within the handle_websocket function. For example, you might parse the incoming message and perform certain actions based on its contents. Additionally, you can send responses back to the client using the websocket.send() method.

Here's an example of handling incoming messages and sending a response:

```
async def handle_websocket(websocket, path):
    while True:
        message = await websocket.recv()
        # Logic to handle the incoming message
        response = 'Received: ' + message
        await websocket.send(response)
```

This example simply echoes the received message back to the client. You can extend this logic to suit your specific application's needs.

To interact with the WebSocket server from the client-side, you can use JavaScript or any other WebSocket-compatible language. In JavaScript, you can use the WebSocket object to establish a connection and send/receive messages.

```
const socket = new WebSocket('ws://localhost:8000/');

socket.onopen = () => {
    console.log('WebSocket connection established.');
    // Send messages to the server using socket.send()
};

socket.onmessage = (event) => {
    console.log('Received message:', event.data);
    // Handle the received message
};

socket.onclose = () => {
    console.log('WebSocket connection closed.');
};
```

With this setup, your Python WebSocket server can communicate with client applications in real-time, enabling dynamic updates and interactions.

Remember to handle errors gracefully and implement appropriate security measures, such as authentication and data validation, depending on the nature of your application.

Building real-time web applications with Python and WebSockets opens up a wide range of possibilities for creating interactive and responsive experiences. Whether you're developing chat applications, collaborative tools, or live data dashboards, the combination of Python and WebSockets provides a solid foundation for real-time communication on the web.

Web application security in Python

Web application security in Python is a crucial aspect of developing secure and robust web applications. Without proper security measures, your application may be vulnerable to various threats, such as unauthorized access, data breaches, and injection attacks. In this guide, we will explore different areas of web application security and discuss how to mitigate common vulnerabilities in Python.

Input Validation:
Input validation is essential for preventing attacks like SQL injection and cross-site scripting (XSS). In Python, you can use libraries like re for regular expression-based input validation, or frameworks like Django that provide built-in input validation mechanisms.
Example:

```
import re

def validate_username(username):
    pattern = re.compile(r'^[a-zA-Z0-9_-]{3,16}$')
    if pattern.match(username):
        return True
    return False
```

Authentication and Authorization:

Proper user authentication and authorization mechanisms are vital for securing web applications. Python frameworks like Flask and Django provide robust authentication and authorization systems that can be easily integrated into your application.
Example (Flask):

```
from flask import Flask, request, session
from werkzeug.security import generate_password_hash, check_password_hash

app = Flask(__name__)
app.secret_key = 'your_secret_key'

@app.route('/login', methods=['POST'])
def login():
    username = request.form['username']
    password = request.form['password']

    # Validate credentials
    if username == 'admin' and check_password_hash(generated_hash, password):
        session['logged_in'] = True
        return 'Login successful'
    else:
        return 'Invalid credentials'
```

Cross-Site Scripting (XSS) Prevention:

To prevent XSS attacks, you should sanitize and escape user-generated content before displaying it in web pages. Python frameworks often provide built-in mechanisms for handling this, such as Jinja2's autoescaping feature in Flask.
Example (Flask + Jinja2):

```python
from flask import Flask, render_template_string
from markupsafe import Markup

app = Flask(__name__)

@app.route('/')
def index():
    user_input = '<script>alert("XSS attack!")</script>'
    return render_template_string('<h1>{{ user_input }}</h1>',
user_input=Markup.escape(user_input))
```

Cross-Site Request Forgery (CSRF) Protection:
To protect against CSRF attacks, you can generate and validate CSRF tokens for each request. Python frameworks like Django provide built-in CSRF protection, but for other frameworks, you may need to implement this feature manually.
Example (Django):

```
{% csrf_token %}
```

Secure Session Management:

Secure session management is crucial for preventing session hijacking and session fixation attacks. Python frameworks often provide secure session management mechanisms that encrypt and validate session data.
Example (Flask):

```python
from flask import Flask, session

app = Flask(__name__)
app.secret_key = 'your_secret_key'

@app.route('/secret_page')
def secret_page():
    if session.get('logged_in'):
        return 'Welcome to the secret page'
    else:
        return 'Access denied'
```

Secure Database Access:

When interacting with databases, use parameterized queries or ORM (Object-Relational Mapping) libraries to prevent SQL injection attacks. Libraries like SQLAlchemy provide secure ways to execute database queries in Python.
Example (SQLAlchemy):

```
from sqlalchemy import create_engine, text

engine = create_engine('your_database_url')
connection = engine.connect()

username = 'admin'
query = text("SELECT * FROM users WHERE username = :username")
result = connection.execute(query, username=username)
```

By addressing these key areas of web application security in Python, you can significantly enhance the security posture of your applications.

Implementing OAuth authentication in Python web applications

Implementing OAuth authentication in Python web applications is an effective way to allow users to authenticate using their existing social media or third-party platform accounts. OAuth is an industry-standard protocol that enables secure and delegated access to protected resources. In this guide, we will explore how to implement OAuth authentication in Python web applications using the OAuth2 protocol.

Setting Up OAuth Provider:

Before implementing OAuth authentication, you need to register your application with the OAuth provider. This typically involves creating an account and obtaining client credentials (client ID and client secret) that will be used to authenticate your application with the provider.

Installing Required Packages:
To implement OAuth authentication in Python, you'll need to install the appropriate OAuth library for your chosen provider. Popular OAuth libraries include python-oauth2, oauthlib, and requests-oauthlib. Install the library using pip:

pip install oauthlib

Configuring OAuth Provider Settings:

Next, you need to configure the OAuth provider settings in your application. This includes specifying the OAuth provider's authorization and token endpoints, as well as your client credentials.

```
from oauthlib.oauth2 import WebApplicationClient

client_id = 'your_client_id'
client_secret = 'your_client_secret'
authorization_endpoint = 'https://oauth-provider.com/authorize'
token_endpoint = 'https://oauth-provider.com/token'

client = WebApplicationClient(client_id)
```

Initiating the OAuth Flow:

To initiate the OAuth flow, you'll need to redirect the user to the OAuth provider's authorization URL. This URL typically includes parameters such as the client ID, requested scopes, and redirect URI.

```
from flask import Flask, redirect, request, session

app = Flask(__name__)
app.secret_key = 'your_secret_key'
redirect_uri = 'http://your-application.com/callback'

@app.route('/login')
def login():
    authorization_url = client.prepare_request_uri(authorization_endpoint,
redirect_uri=redirect_uri)
    return redirect(authorization_url)
```

Handling the Callback:

After the user authorizes your application, the OAuth provider will redirect the user back to your application's specified callback URL. You need to handle this callback by exchanging the authorization code for an access token.

```
@app.route('/callback')
def callback():
    code = request.args.get('code')
    token_url, headers, body = client.prepare_token_request(token_endpoint, code=code,
redirect_url=redirect_uri)
    token_response = requests.post(token_url, headers=headers, data=body, auth=(client_id,
client_secret))

    client.parse_request_body_response(token_response.content)
    session['access_token'] = client.token['access_token']
    return redirect('/profile')
```

Protecting Routes with OAuth:

To protect certain routes in your application, you can check if the user has a valid access token before granting access.

```
@app.route('/profile')
def profile():
    if 'access_token' in session:
        # Access token is available, fetch user data from the provider
        user_data = get_user_data(session['access_token'])
        return f'Welcome, {user_data["name"]}!'
    else:
        return 'Access denied'

def get_user_data(access_token):
    # Make a request to the OAuth provider's API to fetch user data using the access token
    pass
```

With these steps in place, your Python web application can implement OAuth authentication, allowing users to authenticate using their OAuth provider accounts. The specific implementation details may vary depending on the chosen OAuth library and provider, so refer to the documentation for more information.

Remember to handle authentication errors, refresh access tokens when they expire, and ensure proper security practices when storing and transmitting sensitive data.

Building chatbots with Python

Building chatbots with Python is an exciting endeavor that can enable businesses to provide automated and personalized customer interactions. Python offers a wide range of libraries and frameworks that simplify the process of building chatbots. In this guide, we will explore the steps involved in building chatbots using Python.

Natural Language Processing (NLP):

To create intelligent chatbots, you'll need to leverage natural language processing techniques. Python provides powerful NLP libraries like NLTK, spaCy, and TensorFlow that can assist in tasks such as text tokenization, part-of-speech tagging, named entity recognition, and sentiment analysis.
Example (NLTK):

```
import nltk

sentence = "Hello, how are you doing today?"
tokens = nltk.word_tokenize(sentence)
pos_tags = nltk.pos_tag(tokens)
```

Chatbot Frameworks:

Python offers several frameworks specifically designed for building chatbots. Some popular frameworks include ChatterBot, Rasa, and Botpress. These frameworks provide pre-built components and APIs that simplify the process of creating conversational agents.
Example (ChatterBot):

```
from chatterbot import ChatBot
from chatterbot.trainers import ChatterBotCorpusTrainer

chatbot = ChatBot('MyChatBot')
trainer = ChatterBotCorpusTrainer(chatbot)
trainer.train('chatterbot.corpus.english')

response = chatbot.get_response('Hello, how are you?')
print(response)
```

Integration with Messaging Platforms:
To make chatbots accessible to users, you'll need to integrate them with messaging platforms such as Facebook Messenger, Slack, or Telegram. Python libraries like python-telegram-bot, slack-sdk, and fbchat provide APIs for interacting with these platforms.
Example (python-telegram-bot):

```
from telegram.ext import Updater, CommandHandler, MessageHandler, Filters

def start(update, context):
    context.bot.send_message(chat_id=update.effective_chat.id, text="Hello, I'm a chatbot!")

def echo(update, context):
    context.bot.send_message(chat_id=update.effective_chat.id, text=update.message.text)

updater = Updater('YOUR_TELEGRAM_TOKEN', use_context=True)
dispatcher = updater.dispatcher
dispatcher.add_handler(CommandHandler('start', start))
dispatcher.add_handler(MessageHandler(Filters.text, echo))

updater.start_polling()
```

Machine Learning for Chatbots:

For more advanced chatbots, you can leverage machine learning techniques such as sequence-to-sequence models, recurrent neural networks (RNNs), or transformer models. Python frameworks like TensorFlow and PyTorch provide the necessary tools to build and train these models.
Example (TensorFlow):

```
import tensorflow as tf
from tensorflow.keras.preprocessing.sequence import pad_sequences

model = tf.keras.models.load_model('chatbot_model.h5')

def generate_response(text):
    # Preprocess input text
    processed_text = preprocess_text(text)
    # Convert text to numerical representation
    input_data = convert_to_numerical(processed_text)
    # Pad sequences
    padded_input = pad_sequences([input_data], padding='post', maxlen=MAX_SEQ_LENGTH)
    # Generate response using the trained model
    response = model.predict_classes(padded_input)
    return response
```

Building chatbots with Python opens up a world of possibilities for automating customer support, improving user engagement, and streamlining business processes. By leveraging Python's rich ecosystem of libraries, frameworks, and machine learning tools, you can create sophisticated and intelligent chatbot applications. Remember to continuously iterate and improve your chatbot by incorporating user feedback and training it on relevant datasets to enhance its conversational capabilities.

Introduction to game development with Python and Pygame

Game development is an exciting field that allows developers to create interactive and immersive experiences for players. Python, with its simplicity and versatility, is an excellent choice for game development. Pygame, a popular Python library, provides a robust framework for building games with graphics, sound, and user input handling. In this guide, we will explore the basics of game development using Python and Pygame.

Setting up Pygame:
To get started, you'll need to install Pygame. You can do this using pip:

pip install pygame

Once installed, you're ready to begin building your game.

Creating a Game Window:

The first step is to create a game window using Pygame's display module. This window will serve as the main canvas for your game.

```python
import pygame

# Initialize Pygame
pygame.init()

# Set the window dimensions
window_width = 800
window_height = 600

# Create the game window
window = pygame.display.set_mode((window_width, window_height))
pygame.display.set_caption('My Game')

# Game loop
running = True
while running:
    # Handle events
    for event in pygame.event.get():
        if event.type == pygame.QUIT:
            running = False

    # Update game logic

    # Render graphics

    # Update the display
```

```
pygame.display.update()

# Quit Pygame
pygame.quit()
```

Handling User Input:

User input is essential for creating interactive games. Pygame provides event handling mechanisms to capture user input, such as keyboard presses, mouse movements, and button clicks.

```
# Game loop
while running:
    for event in pygame.event.get():
        if event.type == pygame.QUIT:
            running = False

        # Handle keyboard input
        if event.type == pygame.KEYDOWN:
            if event.key == pygame.K_UP:
                # Perform action for up arrow key press

        # Handle mouse input
        if event.type == pygame.MOUSEBUTTONDOWN:
            if event.button == 1:
                # Perform action for left mouse button click

    # Update game logic

    # Render graphics

    # Update the display
    pygame.display.update()
```

Creating Game Objects:

Games typically consist of various objects such as characters, enemies, and obstacles. You can create these objects as classes and use Pygame's sprite module for efficient rendering and collision detection.

```
class Player(pygame.sprite.Sprite):
    def __init__(self):
        super().__init__()
        self.image = pygame.Surface((50, 50))
        self.image.fill((255, 0, 0))
        self.rect = self.image.get_rect()
        self.rect.center = (window_width // 2, window_height // 2)
```

```
def update(self):
    # Update player logic
    pass

# Game loop
while running:
    # Handle events

    # Update game logic
    all_sprites.update()

    # Render graphics
    window.fill((0, 0, 0))
    all_sprites.draw(window)

    # Update the display
    pygame.display.update()
```

Adding Sound and Music:

Sound effects and background music enhance the gaming experience. Pygame's mixer module allows you to load and play audio files in your game.

```
# Initialize Pygame mixer
pygame.mixer.init()

# Load sound effect
explosion_sound = pygame.mixer.Sound('explosion.wav')

# Play sound effect
explosion_sound.play()

# Load and play background music
pygame.mixer.music.load('background_music.mp3')
pygame.mixer.music.play(-1)  # -1 plays the music indefinitely
```

With these foundational concepts, you can start building games with Python and Pygame. From here, you can explore more advanced features and techniques to enhance your game development skills:

Game Physics and Collision Detection:
Implementing physics-based movement and collision detection is crucial for realistic and engaging games. Pygame provides collision detection methods and libraries like Pygame's built-in Rect and Mask classes to handle collisions between game objects.

Game Loop and Timing:

The game loop is responsible for updating the game state, handling input, and rendering frames. You can control the timing of your game using techniques like frame rate limiting and delta time to ensure smooth and consistent gameplay.

Game Assets and Sprites:

Game assets such as images, sprites, and animations play a vital role in creating visually appealing games. Pygame supports various image formats and provides functionality to load and display graphical assets in your game.

Game States and Screens:

Managing different game states and screens, such as menus, levels, and game over screens, is crucial for game flow. You can create separate classes or modules to represent different game states and switch between them as needed.

Game AI and Pathfinding:

Implementing artificial intelligence (AI) for non-player characters (NPCs) can make your game more challenging and dynamic. Python provides libraries like Pygame AI and Pygame Behave for creating AI-driven behaviors and pathfinding algorithms.

Game Data Persistence:

Saving and loading game data, including player progress, high scores, and game settings, adds a layer of persistence to your game. Python's file I/O capabilities allow you to read and write data to store and retrieve game information.

Multiplayer and Networking:

Python's networking libraries, such as sockets and libraries built on top of them like Pygame's networking module, enable you to add multiplayer functionality to your games. You can create multiplayer games by implementing client-server architectures or peer-to-peer connections.

As you progress in game development with Python and Pygame, you can explore more advanced topics like 3D graphics, shader programming, and game optimization techniques. Additionally, there are numerous online resources, tutorials, and game development communities available to help you further enhance your skills.

Remember, building games is a creative process, so let your imagination run wild, experiment, and have fun while creating your unique gaming experiences using Python and Pygame!

Implementing machine learning algorithms from scratch in Python

Implementing machine learning algorithms from scratch in Python can be a valuable learning experience that helps you understand the underlying principles and mathematics behind these algorithms. While Python offers powerful libraries like scikit-learn and TensorFlow for machine learning, building algorithms from scratch allows you to grasp the inner workings and gain a deeper insight into how they function. In this guide, we will explore the process of implementing machine learning algorithms from scratch in Python.

Linear Regression:

Linear regression is a fundamental algorithm for modeling the relationship between input features and continuous target variables. Here's an example of implementing linear regression from scratch using NumPy:

```python
import numpy as np

class LinearRegression:
    def __init__(self):
        self.weights = None
        self.bias = None

    def fit(self, X, y):
        X = np.concatenate((np.ones((X.shape[0], 1)), X), axis=1)
        self.weights = np.linalg.inv(X.T @ X) @ X.T @ y

    def predict(self, X):
        X = np.concatenate((np.ones((X.shape[0], 1)), X), axis=1)
        return X @ self.weights
```

Logistic Regression:

Logistic regression is a classification algorithm that predicts the probability of an input belonging to a certain class. Here's an example of implementing logistic regression from scratch using NumPy:

```python
import numpy as np

class LogisticRegression:
    def __init__(self):
        self.weights = None
        self.bias = None

    def fit(self, X, y, learning_rate=0.01, num_iterations=1000):
        X = np.concatenate((np.ones((X.shape[0], 1)), X), axis=1)
        self.weights = np.zeros(X.shape[1])
```

```
for _ in range(num_iterations):
    linear_score = X @ self.weights
    probabilities = self._sigmoid(linear_score)

    gradient = X.T @ (probabilities - y)
    self.weights -= learning_rate * gradient

def predict(self, X, threshold=0.5):
    X = np.concatenate((np.ones((X.shape[0], 1)), X), axis=1)
    linear_score = X @ self.weights
    probabilities = self._sigmoid(linear_score)
    return np.where(probabilities >= threshold, 1, 0)

def _sigmoid(self, x):
    return 1 / (1 + np.exp(-x))
```

K-Means Clustering:

K-means clustering is an unsupervised learning algorithm that partitions data points into K clusters. Here's an example of implementing K-means clustering from scratch using NumPy:

```
import numpy as np

class KMeans:
    def __init__(self, n_clusters=3):
        self.n_clusters = n_clusters
        self.centroids = None

    def fit(self, X, num_iterations=100):
        self.centroids = X[np.random.choice(X.shape[0], self.n_clusters, replace=False)]

        for _ in range(num_iterations):
            distances = np.linalg.norm(X[:, np.newaxis] - self.centroids, axis=-1)
            labels = np.argmin(distances, axis=-1)

            for i in range(self.n_clusters):
                self.centroids[i] = np.mean(X[labels == i], axis=0)

    def predict(self, X):
        distances = np.linalg.norm(X[:, np.newaxis] - self.centroids, axis=-1)
        return np.argmin(distances, axis=-1)
```

Decision Trees:
Decision trees are versatile algorithms used for classification and regression tasks. Here's an example of implementing a decision tree from scratch in Python:

267

```
class Node:
    def __init__(self, feature_index=None, threshold=None, value=None, left=None, right=None):
        self.feature_index = feature_index
        self.threshold = threshold
        self.value = value
        self.left = left
        self.right = right

class DecisionTree:
    def __init__(self, max_depth=None):
        self.max_depth = max_depth
        self.root = None

    def fit(self, X, y):
        self.root = self._build_tree(X, y, depth=0)

    def predict(self, X):
        return np.array([self._traverse_tree(x, self.root) for x in X])

    def _build_tree(self, X, y, depth):
        num_samples, num_features = X.shape
        num_classes = len(np.unique(y))

        if depth == self.max_depth or num_classes == 1 or num_samples <= 1:
            value = np.bincount(y).argmax()
            return Node(value=value)

        best_feature, best_threshold = self._find_best_split(X, y)

        left_indices = X[:, best_feature] <= best_threshold
        right_indices = X[:, best_feature] > best_threshold

        left = self._build_tree(X[left_indices], y[left_indices], depth + 1)
        right = self._build_tree(X[right_indices], y[right_indices], depth + 1)

        return Node(feature_index=best_feature, threshold=best_threshold, left=left, right=right)

    def _find_best_split(self, X, y):
        best_gini = np.inf
        best_feature = None
        best_threshold = None

        for feature_index in range(X.shape[1]):
            thresholds = np.unique(X[:, feature_index])
            for threshold in thresholds:
                left_indices = X[:, feature_index] <= threshold
                right_indices = X[:, feature_index] > threshold

                gini = self._gini_index(y[left_indices], y[right_indices])
```

```
        if gini < best_gini:
            best_gini = gini
            best_feature = feature_index
            best_threshold = threshold

    return best_feature, best_threshold

def _gini_index(self, y_left, y_right):
    p_left = np.bincount(y_left) / len(y_left)
    p_right = np.bincount(y_right) / len(y_right)

    gini_left = 1.0 - np.sum(p_left ** 2)
    gini_right = 1.0 - np.sum(p_right ** 2)

    weighted_gini = (len(y_left) * gini_left + len(y_right) * gini_right) / (len(y_left) +
len(y_right))

    return weighted_gini

def _traverse_tree(self, x, node):
    if node.value is not None:
        return node.value

    if x[node.feature_index] <= node.threshold:
        return self._traverse_tree(x, node.left)
    else:
        return self._traverse_tree(x, node.right)
```

Implementing machine learning algorithms from scratch in Python not only helps you understand the algorithms better but also allows you to customize and extend them to suit your specific needs. By building these algorithms step by step, you gain a deeper understanding of the underlying concepts and can appreciate the power of Python in machine learning.

Deep learning with Python and TensorFlow

Deep learning is a powerful subfield of machine learning that focuses on training and deploying neural networks to solve complex problems. Python, with its extensive libraries and frameworks, provides an excellent platform for deep learning projects. TensorFlow, a popular deep learning library, offers a comprehensive set of tools for building and training neural networks. In this guide, we will explore the process of deep learning with Python and TensorFlow.

Installing TensorFlow:

Before diving into deep learning, you need to install TensorFlow. You can do this using pip:

pip install tensorflow

Once installed, you're ready to start building deep learning models.

Building a Neural Network:
Neural networks are the foundation of deep learning. TensorFlow provides a high-level API called Keras, which simplifies the process of building neural networks. Here's an example of creating a simple feedforward neural network using Keras:

```python
import tensorflow as tf
from tensorflow.keras import layers

# Define the model architecture
model = tf.keras.Sequential([
    layers.Dense(64, activation='relu', input_shape=(input_dim,)),
    layers.Dense(64, activation='relu'),
    layers.Dense(num_classes, activation='softmax')
])

# Compile the model
model.compile(optimizer='adam', loss='categorical_crossentropy', metrics=['accuracy'])

# Train the model
model.fit(x_train, y_train, epochs=10, batch_size=32)

# Evaluate the model
loss, accuracy = model.evaluate(x_test, y_test)
```

Convolutional Neural Networks (CNNs):

CNNs are particularly effective for image-related tasks. TensorFlow provides layers and utilities for building CNNs. Here's an example of creating a CNN for image classification:

```python
model = tf.keras.Sequential([
    layers.Conv2D(32, (3, 3), activation='relu', input_shape=(image_width, image_height,
channels)),
    layers.MaxPooling2D((2, 2)),
    layers.Flatten(),
    layers.Dense(64, activation='relu'),
    layers.Dense(num_classes, activation='softmax')
])

# Compile, train, and evaluate the model as shown in the previous example
```

Recurrent Neural Networks (RNNs):
RNNs are suitable for sequential data processing tasks, such as natural language processing and time series analysis. TensorFlow provides layers for building RNNs, including LSTM and GRU layers. Here's an example of creating an LSTM-based RNN for text classification:

```python
model = tf.keras.Sequential([
    layers.Embedding(input_dim=vocab_size, output_dim=embedding_dim,
input_length=max_sequence_length),
    layers.LSTM(64),
    layers.Dense(num_classes, activation='softmax')
])

# Compile, train, and evaluate the model as shown in the previous example
```

Transfer Learning:
Transfer learning allows you to leverage pre-trained neural network models and adapt them to your specific tasks. TensorFlow provides a collection of pre-trained models through the TensorFlow Hub. Here's an example of using a pre-trained model for image classification:

```python
import tensorflow_hub as hub

model = tf.keras.Sequential([
    hub.KerasLayer("https://tfhub.dev/google/imagenet/mobilenet_v2_100_224/feature_vector/4",
            input_shape=(image_width, image_height, channels),
            trainable=False),
    layers.Dense(num_classes, activation='softmax')
])

# Compile, train, and evaluate the model as shown in the previous examples
```

Saving and Loading Models:
Once you've trained a deep learning model, you can save it for future use or deployment. TensorFlow provides functionality for saving and loading models using the SavedModel format. Here's an example of saving and loading a model in TensorFlow:

```python
# Save the model
model.save('path/to/save/model')

# Load the model
model = tf.keras.models.load_model('path/to/saved/model')
```

GPU Acceleration:

Deep learning models often require significant computational power. TensorFlow supports GPU acceleration, which can dramatically speed up the training process. You can use TensorFlow with popular GPU libraries like CUDA and cuDNN to leverage the power of GPUs. Ensure that you have the necessary GPU drivers and libraries installed to enable GPU support in TensorFlow.

Model Fine-Tuning:
Fine-tuning allows you to adapt pre-trained models to specific tasks or datasets. By freezing certain layers and training only a subset of the network, you can achieve better performance on your target task. TensorFlow provides tools for fine-tuning models, giving you the flexibility to modify and enhance pre-trained models.

Handling Large Datasets:
Deep learning often requires handling large datasets efficiently. TensorFlow provides features like data preprocessing, data augmentation, and data pipelines to handle large datasets effectively. These tools enable you to load and preprocess data efficiently, ensuring smooth training and validation of your models.

Hyperparameter Tuning:
Hyperparameters significantly impact the performance of deep learning models. TensorFlow provides libraries like TensorFlow Extended (TFX) and Keras Tuner to assist with hyperparameter tuning. These libraries enable you to automate the search for optimal hyperparameters, saving time and effort in the model development process.

Deep learning with Python and TensorFlow opens up endless possibilities for solving complex problems and creating innovative applications. As you delve deeper into deep learning, you can explore advanced techniques like generative adversarial networks (GANs), reinforcement learning, and natural language processing (NLP). TensorFlow's extensive ecosystem and active community ensure that you have access to a wealth of resources and support as you embark on your deep learning journey with Python.

About the author

 Edson L P Camacho is a highly skilled professional with a degree in Technology in Digital Games and a postgraduate degree in Artificial Intelligence. With extensive experience in teaching and mentoring, he has helped hundreds of students to develop digital games using Unity and C#, as well as the Unreal engine.

His passion for learning and innovation extends beyond game development, as he is also a dedicated student of digital painting and 3D modeling for games. He continuously seeks to broaden his knowledge and expertise, ensuring that he can share only the highest quality content with his students.

Edson is a true industry expert, constantly pushing the boundaries of what is possible with cutting-edge technologies and techniques. His commitment to his students and to the field of digital game development is unparalleled, making him an invaluable resource for anyone looking to take their skills to the next level.

One day the prophet Isaiah said...

"All men are like grass and all their glory is like the flowers of the field... The grass withers and the flowers fall, but the Word of our God stands forever."

Isaiah 40: 7-8